Tom,

God bless you in your work + thanks for your last book + its impact on me.

Ron Clark

7/14/11

Am I Sleeping with the Enemy?

Am I Sleeping with the Enemy?

Males and Females in the Image of God

RON CLARK

CASCADE *Books* · Eugene, Oregon

AM I SLEEPING WITH THE ENEMY?
Males and Females in the Image of God

Cascade Books
An Imprint of Wipf and Stock Publishers
199 W. 8th Ave., Suite 3
Eugene, OR 97401

www.wipfandstock.com

ISBN 13: 978-1-60608-483-0

Cataloging-in-Publication data:

Clark, Ron.

Am I sleeping with the enemy? : males and females in the image of God / Ron Clark.

ISBN 13: 978-1-60608-483-0

viii + 136 p. ; 23 cm. — Includes bibliographic references.

1. Church work with abused women. 2. Abused women—Pastoral counseling of. 3. Church work with abusive men. 3. Abusive men—Pastoral counseling of. I. Title.

BV4445.5 .C56 2010

Manufactured in the U.S.A.

Contents

Narratives

Acknowledgments

Thanks to the many people over the years who have taught me about domestic abuse, sexual assault, batterer intervention, and human trafficking. Many have been a part of this manuscript. Ethan Young, Deborah Holten, Emilee Coulter-Thompson, Nancy Greenman, and John Staufer have been very helpful in reading this manuscript and providing input. Christian Amondson, K. C. Hanson, James Stock, and Kristen Bareman have been wonderful supporters in the publication of this as well.

My wife, Lori, has always been a great help to me in becoming a better man. As a partner in ministry and life, she has taught me more than I could ever imagine. Of course my three sons, Nathan, Hunter, and Caleb, have been a joy to raise and challenged me to raise the bar as a parent and, in the future, hopefully as a friend.

Ron Clark
Agape Church of Christ

Introduction

The Creation of Manhood

Both in God's Image

I was a minister at a church that taught English as a Second Language (ESL). We offered this to the community without charge. Our curriculum used readings from the Bible to help them read English. We decided to partner with a local Latino domestic-violence prevention group. They provided the child care and we provided the teachers and location. My teachers were older, retired women who were part of our church. They jumped at the chance to teach. They treated these younger women and their children with respect and enjoyed reading with them.

One woman, Elena, whom we were helping, was working very hard to learn English. She lived in an apartment with four men. She had been brought to America to take care of them.

- We all knew why she was here.
- We all knew what she had to do for the men.
- We all knew that she may not have been in the United States legally.
- We didn't care.
- We all knew that she, the other women, and the organization needed support.

One day Elena was my student. We were reading Genesis 1. She came to the part that said, "In the image of God humans were created; God created them male and female" (Gen 1:27).[1] She slowed her reading, stopped, and read it again. She stared at the page.

---

1. All biblical quotations are my translations.

"Yes," I said. "Male and female are both in God's image."

"Men and women?" she said, cocking her head.

"Sí." I smiled. "Men and women are both in the image of God. Men and women are both supposed to be equal. God loves both the same."

"*I* am in the image of God." She smiled.

"Yes," I said. "You reflect God's glory, and God loves you."

I never saw her again.

I hope it helped.

1

In the Beginning . . . Men . . . Power . . . Violence . . . Sex

History of the World, Part Deux

The Sex-and-Violence Cocktail

In the beginning power existed.

- Power created powers.
- Power was horded.
- Power was dispensed.
- Power was taken.
- Power was rarely shared.

According to ancient texts, gods ruled the world and tried to co-exist in a system of power. In some accounts the Egyptian god Atum brought life into existence by masturbating. Some of the texts suggest that he ejaculated into his mouth and then spit the excess out as creation. Through struggle, life was produced, which brought joy to Atum. In other accounts the Akkadian, Babylonian, Canaanite, or Greek male god became intimate with his female partner. Through these various sexual encounters, other gods were created, life evolved, and beings coexisted.

5

In some of the accounts the male deity went insane and murdered, ate, or exiled some of the children. However, the survivors murdered their dad. In response to this a bloody, violent, and matricidal war occurred. An example of this was the battle in which the Babylonian hero-god, Marduk, split the mother goddess, Tiamat, "like a shellfish" and destroyed her army.[1] Her drops of blood brought life to the earth, including humans, who were formed from this mass to become slaves of the gods. The world that existed now became a nightmare. Sex and violence went hand in hand, arm in arm, cheek to cheek, and sometimes toe to toe. Even more, the sign of god-likeness was displayed in violence and a strong sexual appetite.

- Humans were created in this type of world.
- Humans were created in a brutal and violent world.
- Humans were formed from the blood of the evil, slain victim.
- Humans emerged out of chaos to become slaves of the gods.

Whether humans were created, ejaculated, or molded, the story suggested that in each case the human was a beast created to be a slave. From the beginning, the human was a creature that emerged out of chaos as a by-product of the evil goddess Tiamat. He emerged from chaos into a world of violence.

- He was evil, wicked, an afterthought, a by-product.
- He was to be a slave, a beast, and an object of pity.

In the *Epic of Gilgamesh*, Enkidu was a wild man-beast who did not become civilized until he slept with a prostitute for six nights and seven days (obviously a myth). He is tamed by this harlot, who fed him beer and bread. She bares her breasts at the command of the great Gilgamesh and "laid the beast." The animals flee from the man as he begins to walk on two legs and is finally presented to Gilgamesh by the woman. Enkidu and Gilgamesh become friends, warriors, and buddies. Sex becomes a powerful force that shapes this human. However, in these ancient texts sex and violence are also considered characteristics of godliness.

- In the beginning, the human did not exist.
- The human was created.

1. Speiser, "The Creation Epic," Tablet IV, 136.

- The human was a by-product.
- The human was an afterthought of the gods.
- The human came from the evil goddess Tiamat.
- The human entered into a violent and bloody world.
- The human needed sexual power to emerge from the darkness of chaos, ignorance, and brutality.
- The human's existence was due to sex and violence, because his creators had large appetites for both.

Since the world was created through sex and violence, humans had to embrace this form of existence. Even more, the gods continued to party with their sex-and-violence cocktail. Like a divine still, this cocktail was served throughout the centuries. Shaken, not stirred!

The human's only purpose was to serve. He was a slave. He had no vision and no hope. He did not have power yet he became part of its cycle. Throughout time, the human tried to embrace power, but this power was not designed to make his life better, it was designed to keep him human, an animal, a beast, a by-product, a divine afterthought, and a slave of the gods. This power was withheld and reserved for "the gods." Humans feared and worshipped the gods who created this world through sex and power. In a sense, humans envied the gods who held this power. In another sense, humans tried to grab this power/violence and sex. It was an attempt to enjoy the excesses of "binge drinking" this divine sex/violence cocktail. The human's heroes were hypersexual and violent beings.

Ancient kings were representations of this power. They were distinct from humans because they were not supposed to be like them. When they conquered a city, the king left his statue, his image, or his representation in the city. He was all powerful, all knowing, and in all places. He also manifested the gods' hypersexual and violent behavior. He reflected their glory. The human could only dream of becoming one of these heroes.

Notice, I am using the human in the masculine form. While the original terms included *male* and *female* (humankind), the stories were about men. Male gods brought forth creation, male gods plotted, male gods fought, and the goddesses were the objects of sex or violence. Goddesses existed for fertility and prostitution while gods were involved with power, violence, and domination. The methodical dismembering of Tiamat by her grandson Marduk display the marriage of violence and sex that only a cheap slasher movie could illustrate. She was a witch who got what was coming to her. The aggressive sexual advances by the prostitute to Enkidu suggest that passive men must be "laid" in order to achieve true manhood. The stories are old, but they are current. They are myth, but they are traditions passed down from father to son, from older boys to younger boys. When I was a junior in high school, my father once told me, "You need to find you a freshman girl and have sex—that will make you feel better about yourself." Another time he told me, "You're just a jock. I bet you'd pass up a chance to screw a girl just to lift weights." I guess in some ways I disappointed him. Maybe he was doing what he thought fathers should do. It's the same story whether it is thousands of years old or as fresh as the morning newspaper. However, unlike Enkidu, I became less civilized and more a beast—at least one that was overcome with guilt.

Many millennia later we live in a world that continues to communicate to men the same message. Internet pornography is one of the highest-grossing businesses in cyberspace as well as in the world beyond the United States. In 1997 pornography was a 4.2-billion-dollar-per-year industry. By 2000 the pornography industry in the United States had increased profits to twelve billion dollars per year. Worldwide, the estimate is 57 billion dollars per year. This does not include Internet sites and sales, and underground or pirated materials.[2] Sex magazines and movies, strip clubs, and pimps believe that men are brute beasts, by-products, animals, or an afterthought. All we need to see is skin, or think we see skin, along with vulnerability, and we will do whatever it takes and pay whatever we can to be whole, although we never fill the hole. We are told that we must submit to our urges rather than our conscience and our reason. We, like males during heat, are taught to sniff out females and to be guided by our urges rather than our knowledge of right and wrong. "Boys will be boys," is another way of saying that young men do not have self-control. We are happy to say that "the spirit is willing but the flesh is extremely weak . . ." Our heroes are violent, sexually active, and relationally stunted. Even worse, our heroes who manifest these testosterone-laced lifestyles are those who perpetrate many of our community's crimes. They are heroes and social misfits. The ancient texts continue to affect our culture.

2. Funk, *Reaching Men*, 163; Jensen, "Just a John?" 66.

Women have been taught that men behave in this manner. We are created to be brute beasts, animals, and by-products of our culture, our world, and chaos. We are from Mars; they are not. We are warriors; they are not. We have to fight; they want to love and tame us. We believe that they must take care of us. We are told that males and females are not alike, that we are at opposite ends, and that we don't understand each other. Women must entice men or care for them, but they can't understand them. Yet few can fathom that women must empower men. Single mothers are taught that they cannot be effective parents without a male partner, especially when it involves raising a son. Some feel that women are powerless without men. They are told that boys must have men in their lives to be real men. Even worse, boys are taught that they are not responsible for respecting their mothers, teachers, and other women in their lives.

If a boy has to have a man in order to be a man, then women have little to offer him. She can service him, but only a beast can teach another beast how to be a real beast. He believes that only men can teach him, and that he must become like the ancient human. Therefore, he grows to be another man, another animal, another beast, another by-product. His training is an afterthought, because beasts do not need to think about the future. As Dykstra, Cole, and Capps suggest, "fathers experience difficulty connecting with their boys, in large part because they did not experience such connectedness with their fathers when they were boys."[3] The ancient texts live in the lives of modern men. Instead of sharing power men hoard power, like their gods who they wish to become.

The ancient stories suggested that sex caused men to mature, and that violence and power defined who we were. Together this sex-and-violence cocktail becomes synonymous with manhood. At times women provided a service in drinking the sex-and-violence cocktail. The prostitute did what Gilgamesh commanded and had no choice in the matter. She, like many women today, did what men told her to do. She and they believe that they were helping us become who we were meant to be. However, they are victims rather than service providers. They are the ones who suffer from our cocktail hangovers. If men are the by-products, animals, beasts, then what are the women?

Yet sexual power is not the only force that forms men. Men are taught that our nature is to be violent. We go to war, we sacrifice, we lay our lives

3. Dykstra, et al. *Losers, Loners, and Rebels*, 2.

on the battlefield without question, and we are the first to raise our fists if threatened. Just as we were formed out of chaos and as by-products of a bloody war, so we live our lives in search of that war. John Eldridge suggests that we need an adventure and women need a hero.[4] Yet this suggestion is grounded in a myth concerning males and females.

Male violence continues to be an epidemic in our world today. War, crime, male violence, slavery and human trafficking, child abuse, spousal abuse, rape, and pedophilia are major issues in the United States as well as in the rest of the world. The authors of this violence are overwhelmingly men. The victims are, surprisingly, mostly males.[5] We are our own worst enemies. In addition, men are the major causes of pain and suffering for countless women and children. Men have used violence to solve problems for thousands of years, and we are not any better today for this. We assume that our world is hostile. It doesn't occur to us that there is another way, a narrow way, a difficult way—the way of peace. Maybe it is because we have been told that this is our role in life. The ancient role. The traditional way. The way we must preserve. The way for which we have been created. The way of the beast, the savage, or the by-product.

I have a problem with this "theology of humans" because of what it says mostly to men. While I acknowledge that we men have a history of violence, sexual corruption, and taste for blood, I'm not so sure we should follow the ancient paths; and I'm not convinced that this has made us who we are supposed to be. I understand that history tells us our past, but it does not have to shape and define us. We define history, not the other way around. We created history, rather than its creating us. We do not have to let the myth make the man.

Serving a Different Drink

As a monotheist I believe that there is something better for us. Instead of believing that a group of powerful beings struggled for power through sex and violence, I have found something much easier to believe. A God who speaks, and it happens, impresses me. This God of power, who commands that life not only appear but that it respond, displays ultimate power. Even more, this God also saw that everything was good. In a place of chaos ("formless and empty": the Hebrew language describes it as *tohu wa-bohu*), this God created order. This order was divided into two sets

4. Eldrege, *Wild at Heart*, 7.
5. Earp and Katz, "Tough Guise," 33–35.

of three days, totaling six days, with a day for rest. In a world that circulated stories of war, sex, family violence, and murder, this God created everything with the help of the creation. No power struggle, no need for murder, and no need for sex. It was done with full cooperation from the creation. In a beautiful display of harmony and teamwork God and the creation moved together to produce order out of chaos, good out of evil, and light out of darkness. Instead of Tae Kwon Do it was Tai Chi. Instead of war, it was a dance. Instead of a slasher movie, it was a musical.

The creation of the human was equally as beautiful as the making of the nonhuman world. Humans were not created from evil or the blood of the wicked witch Tiamat. Humans were created as good, even very good (Gen 1:31). God "formed" them, which suggests intimacy, care, and design. Humans were the reflection of this powerful, ordered, and wonderful God. They were the image, statue, or idol that this creator-king left in the world to reflect the divine glory. David, a king, said that humans were, "a little lower than God" (Ps 8:5). They were and are divine kings. They represent power. They are power. They also were commanded to dispense this power to the creation and were expected to care for, guard, and maintain order in this creation (Gen 1:27–28). This is empowerment.

Yet this is where the story changes. Humans were created to reflect this orderly God, this all-powerful God, this beautiful, dancing God who empowers creation to produce its own beauty. As humans developed over the centuries, the story of order, peace, goodness, and harmony weakened while the ancient story of power and sex revived. Male and female were created to reflect the divine glory; unfortunately time, violence, sex, and chaos have eroded that bond and have produced men and women who reflect the ancient gods rather that the eternal God. How would God respond? A world that believed humans were brute beasts, slaves, and by-products of chaos needed God to intervene again. This story came to earth, cut through the fog of confusing myths, and illustrated that one God cared for humans. This God cared enough to create them, bless them, and command them to live in harmony with each other and the world. The story was retold as people left slavery, captivity, and oppression. The story reminded them that God was powerful, and that they were special. Each time the story was told, it broke through their world of despair, depression, loneliness, and oppression. In time, humans once again returned to the stories of violence, sex, and abuse. They resisted this new drink and chugged the sex-and-violence cocktail.

These stories of violence, sex, and abuse destroyed not only the creation but the harmony that existed between God and humans. It destroyed the humans themselves. Men, who forgot that their female partners were also created in God's image, began to subdue and oppress their so-called weaker partners. Men abused their children, who also were weaker. Men oppressed other vulnerable males, nations, and ethnicities. Power was no longer being dispensed. Order and harmony were no longer shared. Even more, women, who were created as helpers or complements to the men, have become the servants and slaves of men. Male and female were both in the image of this all powerful God, but the ancient sex-and-violence cocktail suggested that they were enemies. We men have failed to care not only for the creation but for the created beings who equally reflect the glory of their Creator. The woman, who was taken from man's side to be his partner, has for years been told that she was taken from man's foot to be stepped upon. When male and female unite, is it for better or worse? Is it a partnership? Is it a team? Is she his complement? Do they as a community support and encourage each other to be the best they can be?

Or is she his enemy?

Man in a Grocery Store

I don't know who designed grocery stores, but they were not the same people who designed Home Depot and other guy stores. I know it sounds stereotypical, but I have the hardest time finding things in the grocery store, especially if I am not with Lori.

First, *many females seem to see shopping in the store as an experience*. When I was living on my own or rooming with other guys, a trip to the grocery store was a mission. "You, here, go get all the dairy; you get the meat, I'll canvas the bread aisle, and we will meet back in ten minutes. Ready? Break!" It seemed easy enough. We could get our week's shopping done in fifteen minutes. Twenty boxes of hamburger helper, twenty pounds of beef, dozens of cans of mixed vegetables, bread, butter, milk, and we were done. It was all so simple. We went to the store because we had to.

When Lori and I are out, she says the dreaded phrase: "Why don't we stop by the grocery store and get a few things?"

"What?" I say. "Didn't we do that last week? Shouldn't we have enough in the pantry and freezer to get us through until next month?" It seemed logical to me to hoard supplies and stock the pantries so we don't have to go to the grocery store. However, my wife sees this as an experience. We go down the aisles together, we talk, we compare prices, we pick up things we didn't think we needed, and we have (in her mind) an enjoyable experience. We don't break into teams, divide up the shopping list, or canvas an area (sometimes we go down the same aisle twice). We stroll! The only time we don't do this is when the boys are with us. I,

13

lovingly, offer to sit in the car while she enjoys the shopping experience. Thank God for the Gameboy, DS, and the car stereo.

Not only do many females see shopping in the store as an experience, but they also enjoy the journey to find various items. I understand why they see shopping as an experience. I am reminded of this every time I go by myself to get something she asks me to pick up. Thank God for cell phones.

"OK, I am looking in the soda aisle; they have no juices anywhere in this section." It makes sense to me, because liquids should be in the liquids aisle, with cleaners, detergent, soda, coffee, juices, water: anything liquid.

"Oh, no, honey; juices are at the other end of the store in the . . . aisle." What were they thinking when they designed this store? Why is the frozen bread in the frozen foods aisle rather than the bakery? It's bread! Why are the canned vegetables in a different aisle than the vegetables? They are grown in the soil! It's obvious that the person designing a tool- or sporting-goods-store had no input on the grocery-store design. You can't "go and get" anything in a grocery store. You wander aimlessly hoping to find what you are looking for. In the midst of the free samples, price comparisons, and visits with a store clerk you fill your cart.

One day I had combed the store three times, and finally called home.

"It's in the frozen-foods aisle, right next to the noodles," she said.

"No, I am looking at the noodles; there is another guy who led me here, and we both say that there are no frozen rolls in this store."

"Wait! what store are you at?"

"Safeway," I said.

"No wonder! The frozen rolls are next to the noodles at Albertsons."

"You have the store merchandise memorized?" I asked. I heard the store employee laughing behind me.

"Yes. Now Safeway would have them in . . ."

My wife is brilliant and never ceases to amaze me.

I find that some of us must be a watched group at the grocery store. Every time I go to the store, hold out my list, and look around, an employee stops me. "Hello, sir. Can I help you find something?" Which must mean, "Hello, guy-who-can't-find-his-way-around-the-grocery-store. You won't know where the contents of that list are without any assistance from the workers here. Oh, you can try, but you will wander for the next fifteen minutes and get frustrated. If you were smart enough to bring a cell phone, you will call your wife or partner, and they will tell you where you need to look. However, it won't make sense, and you will need me. We have been trained to see you coming and have been taught to help you. We saw you in the parking lot. I know you hate asking for directions, and that is why I am approaching you first. Yes, the people who designed grocery stores did not have you in mind, because they wanted this to be an experience. But you are on a mission because you want to get home, and you were asked to get one item because she figured it would take you fifteen minutes. So let's cut to the chase and get your item so you can go home where you want to be in the first place."

I get my items and head home. I wonder if the store employees are trained in recognizing males like me on the first day of their orientation. Maybe it is called "Guys in the Store 101."

Then there is the self-checkout aisle. I had the hardest time with that aisle. I would intentionally avoid that aisle. Even if there were ten people in line or a person with a full cart in a checkout line, I would move behind them. Once I stood in line behind three people waiting with full shopping carts. The checker who was in charge of the self-checkout saw me standing there. Four self-checkout counters. All of them empty.

"Sir, you can use this counter," she said loudly. I acted like I didn't hear her. I looked away. The two people ahead of me in line turned and looked at me. One of them, a male, said, "She can take you over there." The checker in my lane said, "Sure, you can go there." I tried to act like I didn't hear them. But they were making eye contact with me.

"Sir," the self-checker said. "Sir, you can use these." I couldn't fake it. Her loud voice startled me, and I looked directly at her. She knew I understood her and heard her. I shook my head quickly as if to say, "No, no. Please don't ask me again."

Then she said, "Sir, c'mon. I'll help you." It was almost like she was coaxing a scared dog to eat some food. I could hear the "It's OK; the big bad machine isn't going to hurt you; I won't let it," in her voice. "C'mon, sir. I'll help you . . ."

So I stepped forward. By the second item it locked up on me: "Please place item in shopping bag area," the computerized voice said.

"See," I said. "It never works."

"Oh, I got it, sir. Let me just scan these for you . . . There we go; all done."

I thanked her for her help and quietly ducked out of the store. I wonder if she learned how to do that in "Guys in the Store 101"?

Since Home Depot put the self-checkout stands in their stores, I have learned how to use them. I can now use the self-checkout stands in the grocery store.

Shopping is an experience for me as well!

Part 1

The Myth of Manhood

One in . . .

One in four females in the United States has been abused by an intimate partner. . .[1]

An abuse-prevention advocate asked a church to host a training workshop. The clergy said they were too busy to spend six hours in this training . . .

One in four women in the United States has been abused by an intimate partner . . .

I had an abuse victim tell me that her pastor suggested she go back to her abusive husband . . .

One in four females in the United States has been abused by an intimate partner . . .

A wife of a seminary student told me that her husband physically and verbally abused her. She felt compelled to go back to him because the dean of the school supported her husband. If she went home, he could graduate and pastor a church . . .

One in four females in the United States has been abused by an intimate partner . . .

A Russian minister told me he did not have time to address abuse— he was too busy . . .

One in four females in the United States has been abused by an intimate partner. . .

Churches sometimes host our domestic-violence-prevention clergy trainings. Usually the male ministers don't attend—only the female ones.

---

1. See Clark, *Setting the Captives Free*, xv–xix, for sources of statistics given here.

One minister stuck his head in the room, looked at what was going on, and left . . .

One in four females in the United States has been abused by an intimate partner . . .

I heard a preacher list the social-justice issues in our country. Spousal and child abuse were not on the list. I wondered why not . . .

One in four females in the United States has been abused by an intimate partner . . .

I had a Christian doctoral student in psychology tell me that women and feminists were exaggerating this issue. I asked him how many women he had talked with about abuse and rape. He hadn't, because he believed that they were blowing things out of proportion.

One in four females in the United States has been abused by an intimate partner . . .

I had an elder of a church, whose mom had been physically abused, tell me that I preached about abuse too much. He felt this was a women's issue.

One in four females in the United States has been abused by an intimate partner. . .

I thought about our first few years of marriage. I had hit my wife. I had contributed to this statistic. I was no different than the men I needed to help. Change is possible, but the memories still hurt . . .

One in four females in the United States has been abused by an intimate partner . . .

One in six males acknowledges having been physically or sexually abused in his life . . .

I met a Christian who loved God, his wife, and their baby. He told me that his stepmother used a one-inch-by-two-inch board to punish him and his five brothers. He told me that one day she broke the board on his head. He thanked God because the beatings stopped that day— until she got a new board. I cried when I got home, and prayed about him. I cried really hard.

One in six males acknowledges having been physically or sexually abused in his life . . .

A young man came for counseling and confessed a struggle with pornography. His first sexual encounter was when he was fifteen. She was a divorced woman at church. She was mad at his dad for preaching about divorce, so she invited the boy over to her house and they had sex. He cried about his shame and addiction. I cried with him.

We prayed, "God, where the hell were you in all of this?"

I thought about Van Halen's song "Hot for Teacher." I feel differently now when I hear the song.

One in six males acknowledges having been physically or sexually abused in his life . . .

A young man came to my office. His wife was expecting a baby. He was scared. He had been molested by his father and uncle and raped by a man when he was eighteen, drunk, and in a hotel. He said that because he had been abused, he was afraid he would be an abuser. He had been praying for a daughter, because he was afraid that if he were to have a son, he would abuse him. I told him abuse was a choice, not inherited. He cried. I hugged him.

He said, "I can break the cycle." He has. He has also helped hundreds of others do the same.

One in six males acknowledges having been physically or sexually abused in their lives . . .

A man who was married and had children came to talk about a struggle with his identity as a man. His first sexual experience was at seventeen with a male professor who met him at a club. I suggested that he was a sexual-assault survivor.

He said, "I can't be—it felt good."

I said that didn't matter. He said he had been ashamed for years. I told him it wasn't his fault. He thought it was his fault. I said, "No. You are a survivor, strong, and a good father and husband."

He smiled. "Yes, I am."

One in six males acknowledges having been physically or sexually abused in their lives . . .

In a newspaper interview, I confessed for the first time in my life a sexual experience with an eighteen-year-old male babysitter. I was eleven; my brother was nine. It set me on a road of shame for many years. It gushed out during the interview.

"You need to talk to someone," the reporter said.

He was right. I did. I am one of the statistics.

However, not everyone speaks out.

2

Who Is the Enemy?

Man Up

As young boys many of us were quickly taught that there are two types of people: females and males. While young, we learn different terms for females: Girls, mommies, ladies, grandmas, aunts, sisters, girlfriends, or women are the people we place in the female group. These titles were used for those females active in various areas of our lives. We also learned that boys, daddies, guys, grandpas, uncles, brothers, friends, and men belonged to a different group. Notice that as male speakers, we do not typically form a compound word with the nouns *boy* and *friend* as we might with *girl* and *friend*. Males were completely distinct from females. Males stand up to go to the bathroom, and girls sit down. (If our dad respected mom, he reminded us to lift the toilet lid.) Boys were designed to have a specific role that identified with our maleness. In addition our roles in sports, choices of toys, clothing, and behavior had to reflect our maleness.

We also learned the differences between boy and girl when we broke the acceptable male behavior code. When we stepped outside of this behavior or *Man Box* as we call it, we were reminded that we were deviating from a certain acceptable form of behavior. This *Man Box* (figure 1) is used in domestic-violence prevention groups with abusive and controlling men. The *Man Box* is an illustration that suggests that males are given a narrow parameter of acceptable emotions. When men are asked what feelings and behaviors are associated with masculinity, a box is created with a list of these emotions and feelings inside (figure 1). A real man, as we were taught, is tough, strong, sexy, independent, and the like.

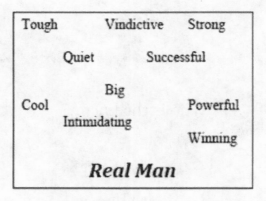

Figure 1: Definition of a Real Man?[2]

The emotions outside of the box, which are opposite those inside the box, are considered feminine (figure 2). Thus, those who are not real men are weak, submissive, dependent, and loving. When we as young boys cried, expressed sadness, or felt vulnerable, we were told to "man up," or to "be a man." We were also taught to "man up" by the criticisms many of our fathers used: "Stop being a sissy." "Stop acting like a girl." "You're being a wuss." "Don't be such a fag." We were taught that manhood or maleness is behavioral rather than biological, and is defined by a standard set of acceptable behaviors determined by other males, females, and society. This maleness, we were taught, did not occur naturally and was enforced by others who understood these "approved" roles that contrasted with feminine stereotypes.

> A second myth—especially when we read popular articles or books about gender difference—lumps all men into one category and all women into the opposite category. It turns out that there

2. Figures 1–3 are used by permission of Paul Kivel (http://www.paulkivel.com) and the Oakland Men's Project, 1983).

is as much diversity *within* a group of women or *within* a group of men as there is *between* men and women. This has been shown to be true in studies of math skills, verbal skills, aggression, and spatial abilities. The *between-group* difference is smaller than the *within-group* difference.[3]

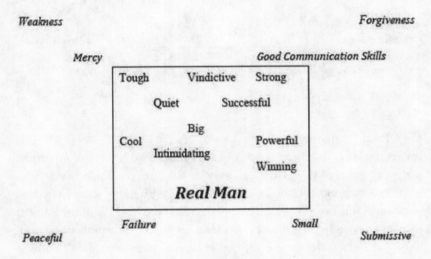

Figure 2: Behaviors Outside the Box

Those of us who heard this advice from fathers, coaches, friends, or other males and females learned that there were emotions we, as budding men, could display. We also learned that those emotions and behaviors that we were not allowed to show were practiced by women and *those who acted like females*. *Those who acted like females* represented a new category that we, as young boys, were told was bad (figure 3). They manifested this new person who was identified by his unacceptable behavior. *Wuss*, *wimp*, *sissy*, and *pussy* were terms used for males who did not "man up." As we grew later in life gay and lesbian terms were used for this new class of human that was created not by God but by other men. The only thing we knew about this "new man" was that we didn't want to be one.

3. Mathews, *Preaching That Speaks to Women*, 24.

Figure 3: Staying Inside the Box

Even though the book of Genesis taught us that God created humans, males and females, both in God's image, we learned that a third category existed. It was the category of the "unacceptable male" who dared to step outside the box. Unfortunately we never knew why this "unacceptable male" willingly stepped outside the box. We didn't know if he was a true rebel. We didn't know if he gave his dad the finger and said, "Culture doesn't determine who I was created to be." We didn't know if he fell, got hurt, cried, and was cut off from his father for venturing out of the box. We didn't know if he liked what the females had and decided he would start a revolution. We didn't know if he was driven to this third option by other males. We didn't know if he was physically or mentally handicapped and had to leave the *Man Box*. All we knew was that he was bad, and we didn't want to be him. He was bad because he didn't know that males and females were separate. He was bad because he displayed qualities only appropriate for females. He was the guy who didn't know when to stand up and when to sit down to use the potty.

Man Up or Else

Because of this pressure, *we could not be ourselves and practice a variety of emotions that reflect the image and glory of God.* We were encouraged to practice only the emotions allowed for males. I find this common in abusive men and young boys. When I ask them to list some of their emotions, I usually hear three: *happiness*, *sadness*, and *anger*. Anger tends to be the most practiced. We learn as boys that we only have a few emotions that "real men" can display. Women, however, are allowed to express many more emotions along with the vocabulary that accompanies them. We, unfortunately, are dispensed a few feelings, most of which lead to anger—the acceptable emotion that males can practice. We are like children who have a limited vocabulary and become frustrated because we do not know what we feel, how to feel, or that we can feel. We use anger because it is acceptable and the only feeling we understand.

Not only have we wrestled with frustration, we wrestle with our enemy. Our enemy is no longer Satan, the opponent of God; it is that group of people who represent behavior we have been taught is wrong. Women and those in "the third group" not only live in the realm we have tried to suppress, but they represent the behaviors that we learned were bad. *Second, we, as men, were taught to suppress, oppress, and control women and those we felt were weak.* In many ways we have been encouraged to do this because we have been humiliated for exploring female territory.

Third, this frustration and suppression causes us to fear women and those we feel are like them. These people practice and so represent behaviors we would like to express, but we have been humiliated for experimenting with them. Having experienced humiliation, criticism, and warnings, we learned that we must reject the "feminine" and stay inside the *Man Box*. We were not encouraged to choose which box to occupy based on logical, rational, and sound arguments. We were not given the pros and cons for choosing to be tough rather than sensitive. We were not educated on the value of the *Man Box*. We couldn't be; it's not a logical choice. We were scared, bullied, and shamed into the box, and it is that same fear and shame that keeps us inside the box. We hate that which we fear. We control that which makes us afraid. We suppress that which makes us uncomfortable. We oppress that which elicits change in our lives.

Finally, *this fear is a root cause for misogyny, homophobia, male entitlement, and abuse of others.* Men fear women because they practice the very emotions that men have been taught to suppress. We fear other men who are labeled "feminine" because they are different from us. We fear people of color because they have been victimized, and those with disabilities. Since we have not been taught to express our feelings, and because we are taught that anger is the most culturally acceptable response to anxiety, we have few options when we become anxious. Since anger has become our socially accepted emotion, we use it well. Because of this, men find it acceptable to use violence, power, and control of others to get their way. We are taught that anger is the response of "successful people" or "real men." When powerful people conquer the weak by using anger and dominance they intimidate and humiliate others. Men find it acceptable to control others and oppress their spouses, partners, children, or other people they deem weak. However, even if we choose not to oppress others, we continue to be silent concerning oppression and violence to others.

Man Up, Man Up for Jesus

In some of the popular books about males and females, men are considered the hunters/gatherers and women the homemakers.[4] While this has been proven to be an overexaggeration of male–female relationships, many people still believe that this explains our gender differences. This is clear even in popular evangelical Christian literature. For example, the book *Wild at Heart*, by John Eldredge, laments the fact that men have become peaceful and compassionate.

> Society at large can't make up its mind about men. Having spent the last thirty years redefining masculinity into something more sensitive, safe, manageable and, well, feminine, it now berates men for not being men. Boys will be boys, they sigh. As though if a man were to truly grow up he would forsake wilderness and wanderlust and settle down, be at home forever in Aunt Polly's parlor. "Where are all the real men?" is regular fare for talk shows and new books. You asked them to be women, I want to say. The result is a gender confusion never experienced at such a wide level in the history of the world. How can a man know he is one when his highest aim is minding his manners?[5]

Eldredge suggests that it is in the nature of men to be like God, but his view of God seems to be cultural. Men are designed to be violent, restless, and aggressive (much like the gods of the ancient myths). In his mind, men are to be warriors, like God. "Capes and swords, camouflage, bandannas and six-shooters—these are the uniforms of boyhood. Little boys yearn to know they are powerful, they are dangerous, they are someone to be reckoned with . . . If we believe that man is made in the

4. Probably the most common book is Gray, *Men Are from Mars, Women Are from Venus*.

5. Eldredge, *Wild at Heart*, 6–7.

image of God, then we would do well to remember that 'the LORD is a warrior, the LORD is his name' (Ex. 15:3)."[6]

Alas, the author continues to suggest that our problem today is that we as men have become *feminized* or *emasculated*. We are restless because deep down we want to be daring, aggressive, tough, and heroic. We should be warriors, not just good boys. These are the characteristics that Eldredge defines as truly masculine.

> To most men, God is either distant or he is weak—the very thing they'd report of their earthly fathers. Be honest now—what is your image of Jesus as a man? "Isn't he sort of meek and mild?" a friend remarked. "I mean the pictures I have of him show a gentle guy with children all around. Kind of like Mother Teresa." Yes, those are the pictures I've seen myself in many churches. In fact, those are the only pictures I've seen of Jesus. As I've said before, they leave me with the impression that he was the world's nicest guy. Mister Rogers with a beard. Telling me to be like him feels like telling me to go limp and passive. Be nice. Be swell. Be like Mother Teresa. I'd much rather be told to be like William Wallace.[7]

Eldredge seems to suggest that we have the feminists to blame for this problem. Instead of teaching us to model the truly great virtues of love, compassion, and mercy, Eldredge suggests that feminists have taken away our manhood by making us become "good boys." Yet most of the men I work with resent their fathers for being the stereotypical male. Most men I know respect the dad who was home, holding the children, and being an example of a good husband.

As I read through Eldredge's book, I couldn't help but wonder if the author received his images of manhood from real life or the movies. His quotation of *Braveheart* and later analogy to *Gladiator* suggested to me that his image of William Wallace and other heroes was influenced by Mel Gibson and Hollywood more than it was by history. His distaste for Mother Teresa and Mr. Rogers slaps women and compassionate men in the face. In an interview with Eldredge concerning his statement about Fred Rogers, he stated, "I like Fred Rogers . . . I didn't mean to set him up as the ultimate bad guy. He's simply a good picture of Christianity reduced to being nice. That would not get a man crucified. That isn't the picture of Christ or of his man. If Rogers were our dad, we would

6. Ibid., 10.

7. Ibid., 22.

carry wounds of passivity."[8] Eldredge seems to suggest that men who are raised by people of courage, such as Mother Teresa and Fred Rogers, grow to be passive, which in his mind seems to be a negative.

Leon Podles, in his book concerning the feminization of Christianity and the church, suggests that the church is not able to attract males because it is too feminine.[9] For Podles males in most cultures reject their mothers in their rite of passage to manhood and continue this rejection of the feminine throughout their adult life. The church and clergy, according to Podles, represent a feminine nature that males wish to avoid. This, in his mind, is an explanation for why many churches in America consist mostly of females, children, and only males who were dragged to the church by a woman in their lives. This sentiment is also popular among other authors in Christianity as well.[10]

It is this very mindset that we are fighting in our ministries against domestic violence, sexual assault, sex trafficking, prostitution, and pornography addiction. This mindset suggests that certain behaviors are either feminine or masculine, and encourages men to resist showing qualities that others, such as Eldredge and Podles, consider feminine. It also fails to address the larger problem in our society concerning misogyny, intimate-partner violence, child abuse, and oppression. Whereas Eldredge suggests in *Wild at Heart* that women want a hero, my wife responded with, "Girls want a hero; women want a man who is a good husband and father." This happens when our cultural and worldly thinking influence our theology. This warps the view of God and requires Jesus to be Rambo. It also inaccurately describes the real issues facing men.

The New Man

I believe that labeling feelings and behaviors as male or female prevents men from becoming like God. I believe this also causes men to overlook the true life and ministry of Jesus. I believe that telling young boys to "man up" or "grow a pair" with the *Man Box* in mind, further contributes to the problems males face in our culture. When the church takes its cues for manhood from the culture, this becomes a problem. Even more, I think that the church will repel men, and women, if we continue

8. LeBlanc, "Wildheart," 34.

9. Podles, *The Church Impotent*, 7–8.

10. O'Brien, "A Jesus for Real Men."

to promote this cultural view of masculinity, since it is foreign to the nature of God, the person and ministry of Jesus, and the ministry of the church.

Feminine language was used in the biblical texts to describe God, Jesus, and the Holy Spirit. The biblical texts were meant to *redefine masculinity*. In a world where gods were both male and female, Yahweh claimed to be one God.[11] Yahweh was a warrior but most often reflected compassion and love, was slow to anger, and was gentle (Exod 34:6–8). While these characteristics were typically defined as feminine in the ancient Near East, Yahweh claimed to reflect these qualities of the divine nature. It was for this reason that Jonah refused to go to Nineveh. "I knew that you are a gracious and compassionate God, slow to anger and abounding in love" (Jonah 4:2). In Isaiah 66:10–14, Yahweh offered to carry Israel in the bosom and nurse them. Yahweh "gave birth" (Isa 21:3), and "comforted" the children of Zion (Isa 66:13). Yahweh is neither male nor female but is Spirit (John 4:24) and reflects a nature that lies in both men and women from the creation (Gen 1:25–27).

Many of the characteristics of God were revealed to men (Exod 34:6–7; Jonah 4:2). The widespread biblical understanding of God as male does not discriminate against women but reveals to North American men a God whose nature is considered feminine in other cultures. In a world that separated male and female gods, in order to supply the "male" and "female" emotions, Yahweh needed no such separation. Yahweh is one because Yahweh can practice both power and compassion. God understood as male brought a message to men, who needed to practice the noble qualities of God's nature in their lives. God was not degrading women but was teaching men how they should behave. God as Father is simply God as a model for fathers. Jesus as the Son of the Father is a model for the church. Jesus as a husband to the church is a model for husbands (Eph 5:23–25). In a world of male violence, God reveals to men that spirituality entails patience, love, compassion, mercy, and faith. When the biblical writers saw God as *he*, they learned that "male" nature was grounded in God rather than in their culture.[12]

In contrast to this argument for the reasons behind the prevailing masculine portrayal of God, Podles suggests that God as *male* was designed to help the nation of Israel mature. For Podles, maturity involves

11. Dever, *Did God Have a Wife?*

12. Clark, *Setting the Captives Free*, 56.

the rejection of the feminine and a rite of passage to the masculine. According to Podles, relating to Yahweh as to one, male, supreme God enabled humans to leave the realm of weakness (the feminine) and move to the life of power, maturity, and manhood.[13] For Podles, this transition was necessary so that the people of Israel could leave infancy (the feminine) and embrace adulthood (the masculine). While this seems to make sense in the cultural realm, Podles' theory does the following.

First, it upholds a misogynist view that the feminine (in the Bible) has qualities that must be rejected in order for people to attain maturity. This can only be supported by a cultural view of the sacred texts, rather than by letting the texts confront and transform culture. Podles' view also fails to mention that cultures practicing this "rejection of the feminine" have a history of oppression toward women and children. *Second, Podles fails to discuss the ancient Near Eastern feminine images (such as birthing metaphors) and traits attributed to Yahweh, such as forgiveness, patience, love, grace, and mercy.* Podles also assumes that Yahweh holds a negative view of the feminine.

For one thing, images considered feminine were used in the Christian Scriptures to describe God and Jesus. *Jesus' touching women and children, his using eunuchs as models of the kingdom of God, and his leaving his family would have made his masculinity suspect in the Roman world.*[14] Many of the characteristics of the Holy Spirit were also considered feminine in the Roman world (love, joy, peace, patience, kindness, goodness, gentleness, faithfulness, and self control: Gal 5:16–24). Paul's use of feminine and masculine family terms in 1 Thess 2:6–12 indicates that the ministry of the church carries the nature of God to both male and female. (Paul describes his ministry team as behaving like a father and a nursing mother.) Feminine and masculine terms were embraced by God the Father, by Jesus, by the Spirit, by the church, and by the Apostle Paul.

Not only were images of and terms for the feminine used concerning God, but *Jesus' humiliation in the crucifixion suggests that he represented the weak, humiliated, oppressed, and vulnerable other category, despised by Roman culture* (1 Cor 1:18–26). The Apostle Paul claimed, as the Corinthians' spiritual father, that the ministry of the church rep-

---

13. Ibid., 63.

14. Clark, "Kingdoms, Kids, and Kindness," 235–48; Moxnes, *Putting Jesus in His Place.*

resented the oppressed of society (1 Cor 4:15). One major emphasis of the early church was social justice and empowering the oppressed. This was to be the identity of the church and its leaders because it was the identity of Jesus.

Finally, *the church has always challenged men to resist the cultural views of manhood which were practiced in the dominant culture, whether in the Roman Empire or in the twenty-first century*. Roman culture encouraged men to have sexual relationships with women outside their marriages: with courtesans (*heterai*) and prostitutes. Wives were expected to be sexually faithful and to raise "legitimate children" for their husbands. Love was something men pursued outside their marriages. Many fathers left the childrearing to their wives or to slaves hired to watch their children (child minders and *pedagogues*).[15] However, the Apostle Paul challenged Christian men to love, nurture, submit to, and empower their wives (Eph 5:21–33), to instruct and raise their children (Eph 6:1–4), and to be a model of encouragement for their families (1 Thess 2:11–12). Paul's comparison of himself to a father who used love in childrearing rather than to a pedagogue who used violence in childrearing was a stark contrast to the typical models of parenting in the Roman world (1 Cor 4:15, 21). Paul also challenged Christian leaders to become involved with their children by choosing a word for "involvement" rather than the common Greek word for family management (1 Tim 3:4).[16] For Paul, Christian leaders were to be family men who were involved with their spouses and children at home.

Many men have been reared to believe that women represent behaviors we are to oppress, avoid, and fear. Our culture continues to reinforce these teachings, and so produces broken men who are frustrated, out of touch with their feelings, and afraid of those who represent what we have repressed. Sometimes these cultural views creep into the church and spiritually affect men who long to be transformed into the image of God.

However, God came to create a new spiritual man, a third category. The new man, exemplified in Jesus Christ, was not distinct from males; he was who men were meant to be. The new man is not an enemy of the female; he embraced the feminine, because from the beginning male

---

15. Clark, "Family Management or Involvement," 246–48; and Clark, *Emerging Elders*, 142.

16. Clark, "Family Management or Involvement," 245.

and female were both in God's image. Just as Jesus united all things to himself, males and females were united in his body, which is the church (Eph 5:33).

Why?

- Because male and female are in the image of God (Gen 1:26).
- Because Jesus freed male and female together (Gal 3:28).
- Because the Holy Spirit unites male and female into a new human (Col 3:10).

Are We Really Monsters?

Living in Fear of the Monster

Many times I will begin a session of my domestic-violence-prevention trainings by drawing a line down the middle of a chalkboard or dry-erase board.[17] On one side I write *women* and on the other side I write *men*. I begin by asking the group, "I want to know what you did today/tonight to come to this class in order to prevent being sexually assaulted." I begin by asking the males what steps and precautions they exercised. Usually the class starts to laugh as the males smile and look as if they are confused. After five minutes I may have three or four suggestions, such as parking by a well-lit area, not stopping to talk to a lot of people, locking the car door, and staying out of dimly lit areas.

I then ask the females what they have done to prevent being sexually assaulted. Within five minutes their side of the board is full, and almost every woman has added something to the conversation. Women suggest that they carry mace, hold their car keys as weapons, walk quickly, make sure their hair is not in a ponytail, and make many, many other suggestions that fill their side of the board. The guys are usually laughing at the fact that they were not aware that this was a complicated issue for the women.

The next part of the presentation is a discussion of what has been written. I ask the men why the women have so much information on their side of the board. Usually the males have no clue. We begin to talk about women, and these men learn that:

---

17. I am thankful for Katz's book *The Macho Paradox* for teaching me this discussion technique.

- Most women are taught from childhood to prepare for an attack by a male.
- Most women consistently think they might be attacked by a male.
- Most women feel they are targets to a male attacker.
- Women live in fear of violence—usually from another male.
- Women prepare to be attacked by a male stranger rather than a male that they know intimately.
- Men don't worry about being attacked, because we are male.

I mention to the group that males are statistically more at risk than females of being attacked by a stranger on the street. However, women are at risk of being attacked by an intimate partner, spouse, or relative. Hopefully the discussion has taught the men that women live much of their lives cautious of other males, especially of strangers.

Myth or Monster?

Why is this true? Unfortunately, the media suggest that women are more in danger on the streets than men. This, however, is not what the research tells us.[18] Our mythology tells us that many female victims are overexaggerating their assault or deserved to be attacked. A young woman attends a fraternity party, drinks enough alcohol to become drunk, and awakens the next morning in a man's dormitory room wearing his shirt. She quietly leaves, drops out of school, and lives in shame. People would believe her, but most would blame her.

Why were you drinking?

Why were you at a frat party?

Why didn't you say no?

Don't you know that you asked for it?

What did you expect to happen?

Few would suggest that it was the male's responsibility to get her home safely. Few would call the men to account. If I were to have surgery, I would sign a form of consent before I was given anesthesia. Why? Because we know that consent involves being sober, clear headed, and not under the

18. Earp and Katz, "Tough Guise," 33–35.

influence of any drugs. However, if a female is intoxicated, many males consider her able to give consent to sex.

When I express that I work with domestic-violence and sexual-assault victims and perpetrators in faith communities, many women share their story of being date raped, abused, or assaulted in the past. They also share that they haven't told others because they feared no one would believe them. I can understand why. I am glad that they feel safe with me, but also am sad that they have had to carry this pain alone for many years.

The silence, shame, and guilt enforced on victims; the "hysterical female with false allegations" myth; and the belief that violent males are typically strangers have created a culture where women fear many males. Some females respond out of fear and struggle to trust males. Others collude with males because they are afraid. Hugh Hefner, Larry Flint, and other pornographic kingpins have women who work for and with them to oppress other women. Some women work with pimps to further enslave other women in prostitution. They are colluding with male privilege rather than empowering women. It doesn't matter that women are part of this process. They are still operating out of fear. It's still wrong, destructive to men and women, and oppressive.

The truth is that most men are not oppressive. Most of us try to be compassionate, loving, supportive, and caring. We realize that we are broken men who are by-products of our culture, of a myth, of a *Man Box*. However, we have learned to be silent. The media have silenced us as well. The abusive men in this world have intimidated us to sit down and be silent instead of standing up to speak out. We watch her pass out at the party while other men carry her to her room. We've accepted the culture's definition of manhood. Many women live in fear of men, of us, and of those whom we have let define who we are and why we should stay in the box. We have become too occupied with idolizing those in the box. Unfortunately, those in the box are the causes of many societal problems.

The men who are trying to live in the box can't see that those outside are being oppressed. We aren't aware that the box is not reality; it's a myth, a construct, an afterthought. We can't see that the new man is a rebel, a voice, a call to change. We can't see that the new man is who God called us to be. Those of us in the *Man Box* fear those outside, and those on the outside fear us.

- It takes courage to leave the box.
- It takes courage to embrace those outside the box.
- It takes courage to keep others from entering the box.
- But it is courage that will come from empathy and compassion.

Slaying the Mythological Monster

Women are taught to fear men, because a small percentage of the male population actually attacks women. We are taught to fear and oppress women because they represent emotions and behaviors we are told are bad. We both live in fear of each other. We both fear the myths. Even worse, we let the myths affect our relationships with each other.

We need to live in reality.

Sex and violence breed in the culture of myths and monsters. They were introduced through ancient stories and have formed a combination of blood, abuse, suffering, addiction, and horror—all driven by fear.

Someone needs to slay the mythological monster.

Who will rise up to take on this task?

Men must confront those who perpetuate this myth. In the past, women have risen to the task of ending domestic violence, sexual assault, prostitution, pornography, and injustice. They paved the way for freedom, equality, justice, and respect. That may be why these have traditionally been called women's issues. However, the abusers, pimps, rapists, johns, consumers, producers, and oppressors are males; it's time that the rest of us, as men, hold them accountable. I'm not talking about law enforcement; we already have that. I'm suggesting that we have communal, moral, spiritual, and emotional accountability.

As a minister I do not need a warrant to confront a rapist—just a conviction from the Holy Spirit. As a man I don't need just cause to challenge an abuser—just compassion for his victims as well as for his soul. As a father I don't need to build a case that a man who masturbates to pornography is no different than a john who pays for a prostitute. I just need to be willing to tear down his walls of hatred, fear, and shame.

God has called me as a minister to proclaim justice and call for peace. Since 1995 I have encouraged Christian leaders, males, and faith communities to slay this monster. Unfortunately, most have patted it on the head, have fed it, or have turned and run. However, more and more men are rising up and standing their ground.

Men who refuse to perpetuate the myth.

Men who respect, honor, and love those like them, who are created in God's image.

Men who are not afraid to reject the myth, the stereotype, the story of violence and sex.

Not an army of one, but an army of more and more.

> In the nonviolent army, there is room for everyone who wants to join up. There is no color distinction. There is no examination, no pledge, except that, as a soldier in the armies of violence is expected to inspect his carbine and keep it clean, nonviolent soldiers are called upon to examine and burnish their greatest weapons—their heart, their conscience, their courage and their sense of justice.[19]

Dr. King was very prophetic in this statement. He knew that the civil rights movement must be led by people who were moral. The same is true as men oppose the cultural views of masculinity and manhood. In order to redefine masculinity, we must develop an army of people who use, not violence, but integrity, love, and courage. Through this we may mentor future generations and slay the mythological dragon that pulls us away from who we were created to be.

It is important that we as spiritual men resist a cultural model of manhood. Our culture and many other cultures present the broken and incomplete model of masculinity. God redefined masculinity through covenant, relationship, grace, and forgiveness, and maintaining and reestablishing relationships with an oppressive people. Jesus redefined masculinity through the humiliation of the cross and associations with the oppressed, the outcasts, and the vulnerable of Roman society. The Holy Spirit redefines masculinity by prompting behavior modification in all people, especially males. God's nature was not manifested only by power and might but by loyalty, faithfulness, and mercy (Ps 146:6).

In addition to resisting a cultural view of manhood, we must also embrace the feminine instead of rejecting it. Women are not the enemy. Femininity is not the enemy. Those who stand for the rights of the

19. King, *Why We Can't Wait*, 39.

oppressed and venture out of the cultural *Man Box* are not the enemy. These are people who, like all males, are created in God's image and also reflect divine qualities that both males and females need in order to exist in harmony and to develop to maturity.

We cannot let culture define masculinity in the church. The triune God has shown males who they are to be. God is our model for masculinity throughout the biblical text and in the incarnation of Jesus. We must allow God rather than our culture to define our nature and the nature of femininity. This also involves embracing the feminine as both divine and part of who we are. Males and females are in God's image. Women are not the enemy. They are our partners, our complements, and another manifestation of God's nature.

There Is a Difference?

When I was a young child, I found that males and females were very different. I knew that males and females were anatomically different during my six-year-old exploratory days and eighth-grade health class. However, I only thought *they looked different*. I had little clue that *they were different*.

In my senior year of high school, I went out with a young lady who was one of our wrestling cheerleaders. We had a nice visit one night on the bus ride home from a wrestling meet. I asked her out for that Friday night. When on a date in a small Missouri town, one does what most kids do: eat pizza and go to a movie. While we were eating, she started to make conversation.

"What type of music do you like?" she asked.

"Boston," I said, "I really like Boston."

"Me too," she smiled. "In fact, most of my record collection is Boston." I looked up at her and laughed, "This is only their second album. Huh . . . You must only have three records in your collection or something?"

She just smiled.

I thought I was funny. If I had been with my friends, we would have told the story over and over and over again. Even worse, before we told the story (for the one-hundredth time) we would have begun with, "I can't believe you said that." Or, "Whaddayah, stupid?" Or even, "Man, that was so funny when you said . . ."

I guess it would have been funny the first five times I said it. But I have a feeling I overdid it. I repeated this story over and over again to the young woman—as I used to do with friends. I thought she was like my friends!

"That was stupid when you said . . ." or "I can't believe you said . . ." or, regrettably, "Three records! Three records! Wow, you must have a great record collection . . . Glad I don't have your collection!"

We didn't go out on another date.

Actually, she never went out with me again.

I thought she would appreciate the humor and the invitation to join in retelling the story.

I was wrong.

Sometimes I forget. I have to be reminded that remarks can be hurtful not because we are different, but because insensitivity is wrong. When I was a child, I spoke like a child. Then I became a man; thank God for empathy and compassion.

3

Playing the Man

I Am Iron Man

It was a hot day at the pool of Gibeon. Gibeon was a city with a tremendous history. Battles were fought, treaties were broken, and murders occurred in this city. It was on this day, as recorded in the book of 2 Samuel, chapter 2, that two groups of men sat across from each other at a well called "the pool of Gibeon." One group were there to support David, the son of Jesse, who was the new king, the young king, the man whom God had anointed and blessed to be the great leader of his empire. He was a great warrior, and his men were devoted followers of this courageous leader. The other group was there to support their fallen king named Saul. Saul was crazy, Saul was paranoid, and Saul was violent. He had tried to kill David because he was jealous of this great warrior—his best warrior. But God had spared the young warrior. Even Saul's own son, Jonathan, who loved David and was himself a great warrior, loved his dad enough to die with him in a senseless battle.

Abner, the commander of Saul's army, had just come off of a crushing defeat from a people on the coast, known as the Philistines. After fighting this enemy nation he alone was left to fight the civil war among his own people. They had taken his king, the king's sons, his good warriors, and his pride. He needed a battle to win and a few men to kill. This might be what the doctor ordered.

Abner sat across from Joab, David's commander. They must have been staring at each other, waiting for the battle to begin. One can envision both sides, like two opposing sports teams, pacing and shaking out their nervous tension while they wait for the national anthem to end and the referee to blow the whistle. These men were ready to prove their worth in battle as well as their loyalty to the king. The unity of the nation was at stake. It was the great civil war.

Will the event begin with the toss of a coin, first pitch, or introduction of the teams with a list of their credentials? No. It was much more than that.

Abner said to Joab, "Let's have these young men get up and fight hand to hand in front of us." The Hebrew word for "young men" means "apprentices" or "young recruits." They were leaders in training. The word for "fight hand to hand" is also a Hebrew word that means "make a spectacle" or "entertain." In some versions it is translated "play the man." However it suggests laughter and entertainment. In essence, these two skilled warriors decided, before the battle started, that they would let the young men entertain them by "playing the man."

That's what they did. Each of the young men rose up, grabbed his opponent by the head, and drove his sword into his side. Twelve men stabbed twelve other men. Twelve:

- the perfect number for the Israelite federation
- the number of completeness
- the number of tribes this war was supposed to unite
- the number of sons of Jacob
- the number of men, times two, killed that day

Twelve-times-two men, in perfect and complete harmony, murdered each other. All this happened so that older soldiers who needed a taste of blood could get fired up in order to shed more. Two crusty old soldiers, Abner and Joab, got turned on or excited when two groups of exactly twelve men killed themselves. They called it "playing the man."

While this happened thousands of years ago, even today men continue to become excited, and fired up by watching men pound each other, hurt each other, draw blood, and sometimes kill each other. We haven't moved that far from the situation in Gibeon. We aren't too different from the ancient Roman culture that promoted the bloody gladiator fights. Thousands of years have passed, but we're doing the same thing and having the same results that they did then. In the story from 2 Samuel, the civil war was violent, bloody, and costly in young lives. What was supposed to unite the kingdom only separated husbands from their wives, sons from their fathers, and fathers from their families. I find it interesting that David, their king, was not even involved in this battle. The story never mentions him. Was this skirmish carried out to impress the new king? Was it done without the king's knowledge? Was it done under the approval of the king, or was this a group of guys trying to impress their leader?

We live in a time similar to their time. Whether it includes watching boxing, ultimate fighting, kickboxing, football, or other sports, in general we men indulge a taste for violence. While we grieve the losses of our sons and daughters in war, we men always seem to be involved in one. We have a taste for violence. We have a taste for pain. Even more, we pay others to entertain us with violence.

> Boxing is an activity in which each of two men, by delivering a series of repeated, sharp blows to the head, attempts to render the other senseless, leaving him lying on the floor, unable to act rationally, defend himself or even stand up. If one of the two men is knocked down and beaten into an only partially blank and helpless mental state, the other is made to stand aside and the contest is halted momentarily, while the damaged man regains just enough strength to stand up and have the beating continue—to the point where he is again lying on the floor, this time completely immobile and functionless. Afterward, the two men embrace in a display of good sportsmanship.[1]

Sometimes I watch fighting, I watch football, I referee high-school wrestling, and I love sports. But sometimes I have to ask myself the question, do I get excited watching men hurt each other? I know it seems trite. I know it seems petty. I know that people think we're making too much out of it. But there's a lesson in 2 Samuel that speaks to us today. Who told us that violence should drive and excite us? What excitement do we get from seeing people hurt each other? Do we enjoy violence?

Throughout the centuries we have developed a taste for violence. The gladiator contests of the Roman Empire seem similar to events that we glorify in much of our language, sports metaphors, and advertising. The Roman Empire loved its gladiator fights, bloody festivals, and sacrifices; yet even the hardened Romans struggled to watch the ultimate

1. Carlin, *When Will Jesus Bring the Pork Chops?* 9.

fights of their day. We forget the damage that violence does, not just on those competing but on those of us who watch.

Years ago I was in Durrës, Albania, and visited its ancient Roman theater. I was told that this had been a site for gladiator battles. The movie *Gladiator* had just been released, and the tour guide told me the story of glorious battles and of the many men who fought there in the arena. Then she showed me the trapdoor to where the lions were kept, and mentioned that the victims had been fed to these animals. We also toured the area under the stadium ruins and saw the ruins of ancient churches located underground. It was interesting to me that the kingdom of Jesus chose to live among the suffering victims, not the glorious victors. I also noticed that the baptistery of this church was in the dungeon of death rather than in the arena of praise. It reminded me that Christianity is about hope in death and suffering, not glory in killing. The Albanian baptistery contrasts with the many religious functions held in stadiums rather than in dungeons and caves.

The Cost of Playing the Man

I met Mark one morning for breakfast. We had been talking about the Bible for a year, because he and I were stubborn and wanted to prove the other wrong. He had wanted to witness to me that I was deceived, and I figured it would take only a few studies to straighten him out concerning the Trinity. A year later we were still arguing, studying, and at times losing our tempers. It was a year when neither was convincing the other, neither was winning the arguments, and neither was willing to change. He was out to prove me wrong, and I was out to enlighten him. Neither of us budged. It was a battle of stubborn wills. We were at the pool of Gibeon eyeing each other and trying to prove who would be right. We had the same king, but we were too busy "playing the man" to acknowledge this fact.

However, this day was different. It was one of those occasional days where our Bible studies had moments of lucidity. These lucid meetings happened when we actually talked about things that we loved. There were those times when we stopped arguing and talked to each other as human beings. There were those times when we had logical, rational, calmer discussions. This was one of those days.

I came to the table at Elmer's Restaurant and saw Mark sitting very quiet. He didn't stand to firmly shake my hand in our way of grabbing each other by the head to thrust our swords into each other's belly. This day was different. He didn't even look up. I sat down with my hand on the sword waiting for an ambush but quickly realized that Mark was in his own battle. He began to talk with me about something that bothered him deeply. I noticed he wanted to share something that was on his heart. As I mentioned to the waitress that I also wanted a cup of coffee, I saw him with his head down staring into the cup of dark java. One thing we warriors had in common was our taste for black coffee. "I hope he's drinking decaf," I thought as I scoped out my opponent. This was a man in law enforcement, a big man, a tough man. I realized that it was time to be a minister, not a Bible scholar, and to sheathe my sword. Something was bothering him, and he needed to share it.

As we began to talk, I realized that this was not a time to dig into the Trinity or whether the Bible I had was actually inspired. It was a time to listen and be the compassionate minister my wife had fallen in love with. As Mark began to talk, he was reliving a part of his history. Mark was a sniper in Viet Nam. He was a good sniper. He could shoot anything, probably because as a boy he grew up with guns. His skill was necessary since we so often need men and women to go to another country thousands of miles away to fight for our local freedoms. Mark began to talk about killing people. The more Mark talked, the more he slowly enunciated his words. This was a different Mark, although it was the same Mark. This was the same Mark who would argue with me about the Bible, and with whom I would argue as well. This was the same Mark who would get worked up and stand on his feet to try to emphasize a point to me that I was not willing to accept. He was the same Mark who was passionate about his faith and about justice. But today, this Mark spoke as if he were in a trance. He was the same but different.

This Mark was reliving a part of his life with which he had lost his passion. This Mark suddenly had tears on his face, which streamed down his black skin. I thought for a moment that they would fall into his coffee cup. Instead, like any warrior preparing for battle he wiped them away.

He looked up and said, "I don't know how God can love me after what I've done."

There it was. I had him, and could see myself saying, "Maybe we can talk about getting out of your religion since they haven't taught you about God's love." But that was not what I was going to say. The time to "play the man" was gone . . . or was it? As a minister I have heard stories from military men and women and know that this is a hard issue to deal with. When you have done this as long as I have, you realize that even if you serve a loving God, and you believe that God is love, you still have a hard time forgiving yourself. Even the best of us who serve a living God know it's hard to forgive yourself. Because we don't forgive ourselves, we believe that this God cannot forgive me. So I listened to Mark. I heard Mark. I talked to Mark.

As Mark began to talk about being a sniper, he said, "Ron, the problem's not just that I killed men. Oh, I saw their faces before I pulled the trigger. I can tell you what they look like. I don't even think it was hard to pull the trigger. I was taught to do it and I did," he said.

"Do you feel bad about doing it? You do know that you were doing what your government told you to do. You do know that you were doing what your government trained you to do? Even if you feel guilt, God can forgive that."

He looked down at his coffee and took a drink.

"That's not the problem, Ron," he said. "The problem's not that I killed them; I can live with that. The problem is what I thought about them, those people."

"I don't understand," I said. "Why did it matter what you thought about them? You just pulled the trigger and did what you were told."

"No!" He looked more intently at his coffee cup. The tears began again, but this time he didn't wipe them away. I was too intently fixed on Mark to notice if they fell near the cup.

"I grew up in the South. I grew up in racism. I grew up hearing *Jim Crow. Nigger.* Any word you can think of for black folks. I grew up hearing that crap, and I hated people who said that to me or my family. I grew up hating white people who use names to belittle me and my family and my race. I swore I would never be like them."

"I understand," I said. "Actually, I don't understand, because I'm white, and I've never been there."

"Here's a problem, Ron," he said as tears continued to stream down his face. "I was one of those people, as a kid, who hated that language, but I became one of those people in Nam. I called them *gook*, and *slant-eyed*, and *chink*; and I pulled the trigger. I laughed later and told the stories like I was killin' an animal. That's why I don't think God can love me."

Wow! What more could I say to help him? Do you think the rest of this chapter will explore whether or not Mark can be forgiven? Can we discuss the theology of forgiveness, repentance, racism, or reconciliation? That would be a safe move, wouldn't it? I could write pages on the salvation of Mark and those like him.

But then that would be too easy.

It is what the church has done for years.

But that's not the issue.

The greater issue is:

- This is what violence does to us.
- This is what it means to take a life and live with the consequences.
- This is what happens when we send men and women away and teach them to kill, to hate, to dehumanize others.
- This is also what happens when we watch violence.

We need a new definition for "playing the man."

Is this what a society of violence creates? Is this what being a violent man is all about? Mark taught me an interesting side of the soldier. I don't see that side of soldiers in the movies, the media, or the heroic tales of men. I wonder if we really understand the cost involved in killing. Even more, I wonder if we understand the cost involved in watching and observing violence.

How does one learn to kill? How does one learn to hate, dehumanize, and degrade another human? One man kills another human accidentally with his car and needs therapy, but another takes a life with a gun and has a celebration. Why are people so different?

Is this what God has created us to be? Is this what it means to be a man? Is this what it means to "play the man"? Even worse, is our definition of "playing the man" really helping to develop men, or is it a return to the ancient tales of sexualized men, gods, and violence?

In order to play the man, do we have to lose something, or will it cost us our innocence?

The Missing Link

From my ministry in abuse recovery and prevention, and research from batterer-intervention advocates, I find that two elements are important in preventing men from using abusive, violent, controlling, and self-destructive behaviors.[2] Empathy and compassion are the missing links in the chain that connects boyhood to manhood. It's amazing to me how these two important character traits can be neglected in the normal growth of males. They exist in females. They are cultivated, encouraged, and nurtured in females. Some of our greatest female role models exude empathy and compassion. Mother Teresa was known for these traits and holds an important place as one of history's most influential people.

Those females who exude these traits also hold an important place in the myth of transformation from boyhood to manhood. Females have empathy and compassion for the rebel without a cause, for the beast, for the hideous monster from the Black lagoon, or for the giant ape. The woman's beauty is thought to change the beast, but the catalyst for change is actually her capacity for empathy and compassion. We, as men, long for this. However, we are blown away when a woman murders her children, abandons her family, has an affair on her partner, or is physically abusive. "That's not normal," we scream. "She must have something wrong if she could do that," we lament. We have been taught—we have been formed by our culture to believe—that empathy and compassion are clearly normal traits for women.

However, when men choose to ignore these traits, we assume that this is normal. Statistics show that males more than females abuse their partners and children, have more affairs, and commit more acts of violence, assault, and murder.[3] Even more, males with higher levels of testosterone, such as professional football players, actors, and other athletes, tend to have more sexual affairs, divorces, incidents of intimate-partner violence, and marital dissatisfaction than those with lower levels of testosterone.[4] Yet we don't seem as shocked when we hear this concerning men. Many of us as men turn our heads, minimize the issue, or assume it is not our business. A president is sexually inappropriate with a member of the staff, violating his oath to his wife. Yet this incident is minimized because "no one died when he lied."

Young men are introduced to manly behavior as a rite of passage. Pornography, prostitution, sexual assault, child abuse, binge drinking, hazing, reckless driving, experimenting with drugs, injuring oneself,

2. Bancroft, *Why Does He Do That?*; Bancroft, *When Dad Hurts Mom*; Livingston, *Healing Violent Men*.

3. Earp and Katz, "*Tough Guise*," 33–35.

4. Dykstra, et al., *Losers, Loners, and Rebels*, 35.

and behaving violently have become the links for many to transition from boyhood to manhood.[5] Many of these behaviors oppress females and vulnerable people in general. While some may suggest that these behaviors may not be directly encouraged, they exist in a culture that promotes their practice while many other males are silent. Even more, we believe it is normal and necessary for boys to practice many of these behaviors in order to become men.

Society also places a tremendous burden on males as a group. Young males pay higher costs for automobile insurance, face lower life expectancies, engage in more risky behaviors, and show higher high-school dropout rates than females.[6] We are at risk because we have followed the ways of the ancient ones. Sex and violence are our gods, who in turn enslave us. We are an afterthought, a by-product, expendable. Instead of rising up and crying out for change, we break the chain that connects boyhood to manhood, we break links of empathy and compassion. Therefore we sever our past attachment to the feminine, attachments to those who have the ability to nurture, love, and help us mature emotionally.

Other ancient cultures believe that the chain must also be broken between boyhood and manhood. The rites of passage for men are an attempt to isolate the young boy from his mother and anything feminine. The transition must be severe in order to drive away any resemblance of a female in his life. Empathy and compassion leave, and we fill their void with the sex-and-violence cocktail. In cultures continually at war with other tribes, this is deemed necessary. However, in cultures where there is peace, violence continues as the norm. Currently in America, families of returning GIs still experience stress when the GIs return home from war. Sometimes peace is established when the soldiers are deployed again. Clearly, training people to be violent will cause problems in a society that seeks peace. Training in violence also continues to cultivate an environment where women, children, and generally the vulnerable are oppressed.

The concept of separating the boy from anything feminine is not healthy. While it is practiced in many cultures, it is a reflection of the ancient myths in which prostitutes, war, and oppression of the weak are thought to civilize men. The separation of boys from the feminine also

5. Earp and Katz, "*Tough Guise*," 33.
6. Katz, *The Macho Paradox*, 21–22.

removes two important ethical qualities needed for the survival of the human race. Empathy and compassion are necessary moral qualities for developing normal human beings and for maintaining harmony in society. They are central qualities for developing ethics in our spiritual lives.[7]

Rise Up, O Men of God . . . or Else

Whereas a rejection of the "feminine" concerns me, I am equally concerned at the response of some male Christian authors who have, unfortunately, had their view of manhood clouded by their culture and the myths of the ancients. First, *I find that many leaders and influential thinkers in the evangelical Christian community are rejecting anything "feminine."* This may be caused by a "fear of the women." With the introduction of the birth-control pill, women have begun to feel empowered concerning sexuality, birth, and marriage. It is no longer the role of the woman to prevent pregnancy; it is both our responsibilities. Men can no longer "impregnate" women and abandon them to spend their lives "with the kid." Women have been given choices.

Some in the evangelical faith community express this fear in their treatment of women in ministry and by slowness in addressing domestic abuse and its role in divorce. Over the years I have been active in training faith-community leaders to address domestic violence, sexual assault, and other forms of female oppression. Sadly, few males attend these trainings. Those that do, however, have a tremendous impact on the health of their congregations. The Association of Marriage and Family Ministries has been a great supporter in our efforts to help marriage-and-family ministries address dysfunction, abuse, and male violence in homes and in churches. In creating a team to address this sin, we have found acceptance and support. However, most churches are still ill equipped or unwilling to hold men accountable for their sexist, violent, and controlling behavior. Few seminaries even require the students to learn about domestic violence, sexual assault, and other forms of family violence. Yet clergy are the most sought-out resources for help by women who are in abusive relationships.

This fear of women among some evangelical leaders is also expressed by our stance on "the family" by opposing divorce without ad-

7. Thomas, *Moral Development Theories*, 155.

dressing abuse and dysfunction. We believe that people "throw away marriages" without acknowledging the agony that many people face in divorce and reconciliation. In addition to this, we do not address the real problem. Women, feminism, and secular agencies are blamed for empowering women to leave marriages supporting abortion, and attacking the family. However, the majority of families fall apart not because of divorce, or because men aren't studs, or because women aren't submissive enough; they fall apart because many husbands and fathers fail to practice empathy and compassion. Men are the major reason marriages end. Therefore, Christianity must call men to be the kind of men God has called them to be.

Second, in addition to a rejection of the feminine, *there has been a movement in the evangelical Christian community to revive the "true calling of men."* Authors such as Eldredge, Podles, Mark Driscoll, Paul Coughlin, and David Murrow suggest that the problem with the church is "feminized men."[8] In Murrow's book *Why Men Hate Going to Church*, he suggests that the church has become boring to men, has condemned the masculine spirit, and has lost touch with what men really want.[9] Podles suggests that the church is effeminate because clergy, church doctrine, the overwhelming presence of women, and image of Jesus constructed by the feminine church is not appealing to men.[10] In their view the mission of the church seems to call men to embrace a nature that they have been taught to reject. For these authors the church doesn't reach men because it's feminine and concerned with "womanly" matters. In some way "real men" are too manly to be attracted to this church. As Podles suggests, "true men" have made a break with the feminine (as he believes they should) and have rejected anything that models this behavior. Why not reject the feminized church, as Podles and others suggest? Therefore their solution is that the church must become manly (as it was meant to be). The church must focus on the things of men. The church must redefine Jesus as a true man, an ultimate fighter, a warrior, a hunter, and restless soul. The rejection of all things womanly is the new messiah that the authors of the "new masculinity" believe will attract men and save the church.

---

8. Eldredge, *Wild at Heart*, 7–8; Podles, *The Church Impotent*, 5–6; Murrow, *Why Men Hate Going to Church*, 26; and O'Brien, "Jesus for Real Men."

9. Murrow, *Why Men Hate Going to Church*, 26.

10. Podles, *The Church Impotent*, xii.

Yet these authors fail to address the research that indicates that clergy and males with lower levels of testosterone are more satisfied with their marriages and their lives.[11] They also seem to be silent concerning men's violence against women, children, and vulnerable others. While they indirectly disagree with this violence and oppression, I find that they do not address the root causes of this violence—fear of and disrespect for women, the feminine, and weakness.

When I have spoken of my concerns at conferences or workshops, some advocates of these authors' printed works remind me that these men would never support domestic abuse and oppression. However, they don't have to. By their silence and unwillingness to condemn the actions and attitudes associated with male oppression, they foster an environment conducive to male entitlement. Without acknowledging that misogyny creates many of the problems caused by males, they continue to suggest that those who listen to and support women are emasculated. By reinforcing the *Man Box* behavior, they cultivate the male stereotypes defined by culture rather than God. By their disdain for the "feminine," they create an environment where abuse, power and control, and oppression can thrive. By their language of violence and oppression, they reintroduce the myths of Babylon, Egypt, and other cultures competing with God's ideals for males and females. This is why so many abuse-prevention advocates (Christians included) suggest to me that what these authors are doing is reinforcing old stereotypes concerning how men should treat women and other men who do not fit into their culture's view of masculinity. They reinforce the ways of the ancients, whose heroes were created by men who idealized violence, hypermasculinity, and sex. They in turn collude with their culture in the name of Christianity. They are similar to the madam who supports her pimp by patting "her girls" on the head. "Now girls, you remember that you're showing these men a good time by supporting oppressive stereotypes. They deserve it, because boys will be boys . . ."

Finally, reinforcements of stereotyped masculinity *cause men to be oblivious to the real reason they do not go to church*. Men and women between the ages of twenty and thirty are leaving the church in large numbers. They believe that the church is not relevant to their lives. They are educated and feel that the church doesn't challenge them. They are committed to social justice and believe that the church is oblivious to

11. Dykstra, et al., *Losers, Loners, and Rebels*, 35.

this issue (an issue Podles suggests is mainly important to females).[12] They are leaving because the church is not reaching those outside the church community. In addition to this, the church was never called to imitate its culture. The church has been called to transform culture. Men who reflect the image of their culture must be called to reflect the image of Yahweh, Jesus, and the Holy Spirit. The authors of the new masculinity seem to forget that the apostles and Jesus called the church to redefine masculinity and flew in the face of cultural definitions of manhood. In an empire where gladiator fights were common, the church spoke against these events and called for peace.

However, the new authors of Christian masculinity have also constructed an enemy. Philosophers call this a "straw man." In this method of arguing, one constructs a caricature of an opponent, or a faulty version of an argument one opposes (a straw man) and proceeds to tear down the opposition with one's own arguments and answers, resulting in victory. However, the argument fails when we realize that the assertions toppled a straw man. The straw man of the authors under discussion is feminism. Women and anyone feminine are blamed for men's choosing not to follow Christ or attend church. Elderedge reinforces this as he wrote that men view pornography because they are intimidated by women.[13] The rest of the research on pornography suggests that the root cause of this issue is misogyny, oppression, and devaluing women.[14] Robert Jensen suggests that the three themes of pornography are that: 1) all women want sex from all men at all times; 2) women naturally desire the kind of sex that men want, including sex that many women find degrading; and 3) any woman who does not at first realize this can be turned on with a little force.[15] This is attributed to be the reason that men view pornography: disrespect for women. The authors of the new masculinity want us to feel sorry for men who look at naked flesh and blame women for the failings of these men. However, this is a straw-man (or straw-woman) argument. Men make choices and decisions and should be held accountable for their actions. The church must once again call men to choose to be different. This is the call to repentance.

12. Podles, *The Church Impotent*, 18.

13 Elderege, *Wild at Heart*, 44.

14. Funk, *Reaching Men*, 165.

15. Jensen, "Just a John?" 66.

- Men choose to look at pornography.

- Men choose to lust after women.

- Men choose to believe that a woman who is nice to them wants them sexually.

- Men choose to rape and sexually violate women.

- Men to choose to control and coerce other women, children, and vulnerable people.

- Men choose to physically assault women.

- Men choose to withhold emotional support from their partners, children, and others.

- Men choose to neglect their wives, children, and others.

- Men choose to disrespect others due to their race, gender, looks, or status in society.

- Men choose not to love, repent, or change.

- Men, however, also *choose to* love, repent, and be different.

Likewise the church is called to engage our culture and teach men what God has called them to be. As we engage our culture, we must teach men that they have a choice and that they can choose to reflect the image of our eternal God or the image of the temporary society where we live. We do not need the cultural views of masculinity and manhood, because they are part of this temporary realm.

I meet few men who lament that the church is for "wusses." I meet no men who tell me that their father was not a "stud" and therefore not the cause of their issues. However, I have yet to meet a man who would resent his father being like Mr. Rogers. I meet boys who wish that their dads were tougher, but as the boys grow to be men they love their dads for who they are. I do meet men who complain because their fathers neglected them, did not hold them, were not available for them physically or emotionally, or did not show interest in their lives. I've never had a man call me a sissy for wrestling with my boys, kissing them, or taking them with me wherever I go (unless men have called me a sissy behind my back). I have never had a man (to my face, at least) laugh at me for holding other people's babies or playing with their kids. I usually hear, "I wish my dad would have done that with me," to which I reply, "Me, too; but we can both be the ones to break the cycle." Or at least we can keep from breaking the chain, and reinforce the links of empathy and compassion.

We are letting men off the hook. Men are in a culture that, like the ancient myths, tells them they are by-products, afterthoughts, and expendable. The culture does what it has done for thousands of years; it tells them that sex, violence, and oppression are their roles in life, their obligation, and their highest forms of enjoyment. The culture, like the soldiers at Gibeon, encourages them to "play the man," to follow the way of the ancients, and to fulfill the destiny of the man. When those who "play the man" fall victim to its destruction, the culture, like the soldiers at Gibeon, cares little for their lives. They are only a form of entertainment, a spectacle, an afterthought, a by-product, an expense.

They break the chain but not the cycle.

Life continues as it always has.

But the future is not yet!

I am concerned at the attempts of the authors of the new masculinity and the response of the Christian church. First, *the church is to redefine culture and masculinity, not the other way around.* Second, *our culture has a tremendous problem with male violence and the oppression of women, children, and vulnerable others.* The church is called to confront this behavior both with men and women. Therefore we must avoid the roots of this oppression, which are misogyny, entitlement, male privilege, and violence. Third, *this oppression contributes to racism, something that the church has been slow to address.* Unless we confront male privilege, which is prevalent in our culture, we will never remove racism. All oppression stems from fear. Finally, *Jesus was viewed by Roman culture as effeminate, weak, and powerless.* Roman males would have viewed Christianity as weak since Jesus was humiliated on the cross and associated with those in the "feminine" class (the outcasts, the poor, the oppressed, the humiliated, and the like). Over the centuries, many philosophers, historians, and writers have condemned Christians and Christianity because of our emphasis on love, compassion, forgiveness, and social justice. Yet we have continued to transform people in every generation. At Corinth, Paul claimed that the majority of the church came from the outcasts and oppressed in society (1 Cor 1:26). However, Christianity still attracted males, not because it reflected culture, but because it redefined masculinity by confronting its culture.

My First Experience as a Racist

When I was in third grade, I went to Bonham Elementary School in Abilene, Texas. My dad was a B-52 bomber pilot stationed at a nearby base while he was on a tour of duty in Vietnam. My mom tried to raise two boys while he spent a year in Vietnam on his mission for the United States Air Force. My dad was somewhat racially prejudiced even though the military discouraged expressing prejudice. However, "blacks" were his targets. I somehow had friends who were African American and never saw myself as prejudiced, just as few third-grade boys would think that they themselves were prejudiced.

One day Bobby, Mikey, and I were sent to clean the boys' bathroom. Someone had thrown trash on the floor, spit on the walls and mirrors, and left mud in the sinks. The teacher sent us to do the dirty job since no one was willing to fess up to it. As Bobby, Mikey, and I started the task of picking up the trash, we talked and joked around, as any kids would do when faced with cleaning someone else's spit off of the wall.

"I know who did this, "Bobby snarled.

Mikey and I wondered who this was, and how Bobby had access to this important information. Bobby now became the authority in our search for a scapegoat, an offender, a target. Bobby had our full attention, and he seemed to be an oracle of the most high god, speaking words of truth and justice. We put our brooms down.

"Who was it?" Mikey asked.

"It was those Mexcans [*sic*]; it was those damn Mexcans," Bobby said slowly as he tried to annunciate each word.[16] "My mom says those damn Mexcans tear everything up. I know it was those damn Mexcans."

Mikey and I looked at each other and laughed because he had said *damn*; we were unaware that we were being introduced to a blatant act of racism. Instead, we smiled and laughed that Bobby was cussing.

"Benny," I said, as Mikey and I laughed.

"Yeah," Bobby said. "Benny—he's one of them." Benny was the most popular Latino male in our class. We all liked Benny. He was quiet, smiled a lot, was a good kickball player, and worked hard at school. Benny never got in trouble at school. However, none of that mattered now.

"Yes, Benny," Bobby mumbled as he looked at the spit on the mirror.

"Yes. Benny, that damn Mexcan, did this."

---

16. The spelling "Mexcan" reflects our childhood pronunciation of *Mexican*.

This was all that was said. We went back to work and joked around as most third-grade boys do. We cleaned up the spit, the mud and the trash. It was as if the conversation never happened. Bobby had ended it as fast as he had started it. We assumed that the self-appointed source of wisdom had spoken the final word.

That night I went home and retreated to my room. I wanted to do what most third-grade Texan boys did. I played with my Alamo toy set. My soldiers were set up and stationed around the San Antonio fort. My favorite soldier (representing me) stood next to Davy Crockett (who in my mind looked a lot like John Wayne), and together we held the famous last stand at the Alamo. Only this time, the battle was personal. We fought the "damn Mexcans."

"Hey," my mom said. "Don't say that—you don't talk about people that way." She peeked her head into my room. She was attempting to address my language, but it fell on deaf ears. I quietly played and used the newfound phrase that gave life to these inanimate soldiers.

"Kill those damn Mexcans!" I laughed as Davy and I rewrote history and won the battle of the Alamo. In my mind, these plastic figures were still objects, but they had a name, a persona, a face. "Yes," I thought. "We rewrote history and I was part of it; we killed them all."

At school the next day, things were normal. We all worked on our writing, listened to the teacher, laughed at the kids who picked their noses and put their fingers in her mouths thinking no one was looking. We all talked quietly and colored our pictures of the Alamo. During recess Mikey and I went to Bobby and said, "Hey that was funny when you said 'damn Mexcans.'" Bobby smiled and began to curse them and cuss even more. He blamed them for trashing the bathroom and then started using Benny's name. After five minutes, he and Mikey were laughing along with the other kids who'd gathered around to hear Bobby cuss. Not me. I had turned and begun to march over to another group of kids.

"Where ya goin', Ronnie?" Bobby yelled.

"I'm going to kill that damn Mexcan," I screamed.

"Cool," the kids said, and formed a pack behind me as I chanted through clenched teeth, "Damn Mexcan. Kill that damn Mexcan." I marched over to Benny who was playing on the swing with other kids.

"Hi," he said as he smiled at me.

"You damn Mexcan: you tore up the bathroom and made us work. I hate you . . ." I said as I grabbed his shirt.

I don't remember the look on his face, I don't remember the other kids' faces, I don't even know why a teacher did not intervene. I remember his white shirt with a dark brown design coming off as I grabbed him. I grabbed his white undershirt and swung him around once and threw him to the ground. His brown pants and brown cowboy boots looked just like I had imagined the Mexican army wearing as they stormed the Alamo. Benny hit the ground hard. I threw his shirt down on the ground. I don't remember if I said anything or what the crowd of kids was yelling. It was an act of rage provoked by my own sense of anger, fear, and stupidity. I didn't think!

Then I heard a sound that seemed to stop everything. The rage that was in me was suddenly transformed into guilt, sadness, and sorrow. I heard a whimper and then Benny cried as he pushed himself up to face me. Everything changed. The tears rolled down his cheeks and no one said a word. No one intervened. It was just me and Benny.

"I'm sorry, Benny," I said as I tried to help him stand and dusted off his shirt. "I'm sorry, I'm sorry, I'm sorry," I begged as I gave him his shirt.

"Please don't cry."

"OK, Ronnie," he said as he wiped the tears away and smiled.

All the rage, the anger, the hatred was replaced by guilt, sadness, and sorrow. I don't know if it was empathy, but it was the worst feeling I could remember as a child. The rest of the day I apologized to Benny. We weren't the best of friends, but I never said that horrible phrase again (at least not that I can remember). Somehow this act of rage taught me something about myself. Was I a racist? Was I a product of racial pressure? Was I prejudiced?

As I look back on that experience, I realize how powerful that moment has been for me. Maybe it has formed who I am now. I cried when I wrote this down, because I have never told anyone this story. I've never told my wife or my sons. I've never shared this with churches where I have preached. Maybe the shame has kept me silent about racism. Maybe racism and prejudice remind me of who I am or was or could have been. I visited that school in 2009 while speaking at a university in the city. I went to the playground and saw the spot where it happened. A flood of emotion came over me. It still hurts.

I don't know what happened to Benny. I wonder how many times he has had to smile and say, "OK" since then. I know Bobby was the one who trashed the bathroom, and that the teacher thought Mikey and I would be a good influence on him if we had to clean up his mess. How interesting! Characteristics of racism and social pressure are seen throughout this story. I was not a racist. Bobby was not a racist. The kids were not racists. We were empty vessels, sponges, and open books waiting to be completed. Someone told Bobby that Latinos were scapegoats. Someone also told me. Toy makers unintentionally helped to fuel the fires of Texas pride over a war that had happened one hundred years before. As Latinos moved farther north, the "American fort" had to take a last stand. The school I attended was named after James Butler Bonham, one of the Texas leaders who died at the Alamo. Hatred and rage were due to a false sense of justice. Cowards targeted good people because they were afraid to admit their own sins.

I have also learned something else about racism. Compassion can destroy racism. Empathy kills prejudice. Hearing Benny cry moved me to hurt *with* him. I had hurt Benny and felt sorry for that. Somehow, thank God, I had learned that hurting others was not good. Unfortunately my hands had administered this pain. I wish I could have learned this lesson without inflicting pain on an innocent boy. Maybe this is the source of my guilt and shame concerning the story, and the reason for my return to the playground. Maybe this story will help others gain empathy and compassion without being themselves a source of suffering. I had hurt Benny and felt sorry. Somehow that memory is deep in my subconscious and has kept me from unleashing the raging monster that was present on the playground. Or at least I have kept this monster subdued.

Years later one of my sons and I met a Russian family living in Portland. He was teaching English to them, and they invited us to stay for dinner. Natalia is an excellent cook and Victor a great host. We sat across from one another and talked about living in the 1970s, before the Berlin Wall fell. We talked about Soviets' and Americans' being afraid of each other and being taught to hate each other. From their perspective during the '70s and '80s they had very little, and we had everything. From my perspective during the '70s and '80s, they were out to take our faith and our possessions.

On the drive home my son asked me about our conversation, and why both countries were at odds. I explained to him that our governments deemed each other the enemy. I told him about the Red Scare. Our missiles had been pointed at each other; we had boycotted each other's Olympics; we were each other's enemy in sports, and as a child I had pretended that all my enemy toy soldiers were Russians. Everything revolved around beating the Russians. In college track and cross-country, we firmly believed all Eastern Bloc runners (male and female) used steroids. The movie *Rocky IV* still reinforced the old stereotypes about Russians when I was a college graduate. It was the height of paranoia, and fear mixed with nationalism and racism.

My son shook his head. "Sounds stupid," he said.

I think he's right.

It was.

It is.

We were.

He's a sponge, an empty vessel, a book waiting to be filled.

I pray that his pages will be filled with empathy and compassion.

Empathy and compassion are important moral qualities in the development of all humans. They are necessary for the emotional, spiritual, and physical development of those created in the image of the eternal God. In the Sermon on the Mount Jesus stated:

> You have heard that, 'You should love your neighbor and hate your enemy.' But I tell you that you should love your enemies and pray for those who attack you, so that you may be children of your Father who is in heaven; who makes his sun rise on the evil and the good, and sends rain on the just and on the unjust. If you love those who love you, what reward do you have? Don't tax collectors do the same? If you embrace/greet only your brothers and sisters, is that any more than other people do? The Gentiles do the same? You need to be mature, as your heavenly Father is mature. (Matt 5:43–48)

The Greek word usually translated "perfect" in Matt 5:48 is the word that means "mature" or "complete." Jesus stated that God the Father displays maturity by loving unconditionally. When males and females love unconditionally, they are spiritually and emotionally mature—like their God and Father. This is especially challenging to men who are fathers. They must model maturity to their children and to others by loving unconditionally and being open to accepting all people, good or bad.

Unfortunately our society gives permission for only females to be loving, accepting, and in this case, spiritually and emotionally mature. As the links of compassion and empathy are shattered when a male transitions from boyhood to manhood, the connections both to the feminine and to God are broken. The male has difficulty maturing and reflecting the true image of God, because empathy and compassion are necessary for one to love unconditionally. Does it surprise us that so many males struggle with misogyny, racism, hopelessness, power and control, and an inability to form relationships with others? Does it surprise us that culturally accommodating males is valuable not only in a world that binges on the sex-and-violence cocktail, but also in a society that distills the powerful drink?

We need a new definition for "playing the man."

We need a new definition of a "rite of passage."

We need a new group to redefine masculinity.

We need a church that reflects spiritual and emotional maturity.

We need to think outside the *Man Box.*

Life Can Be Bogus

Bogus, Bogus! Life can be bogus!

I saw a great evil under the sun . . .

Women and children were in danger from the men who were supposed to love them. But we convinced them that they needed to fear the stranger. While men were more in danger from other men and strangers, we told them to fear women, children, and those who threatened our masculinity.

From my training in abuse recovery and prevention I have learned that . . .

One in four women was being physically beaten by a male lover . . . at least by someone who said he loved her.

Children were being abused by their fathers and stepfathers.

One in six boys was being molested and abused by a caregiver.

Few pedophiles are convicted of this crime and serve jail time.

My city (Portland, Oregon) had the highest number of strip clubs per capita in the United States.[1]

Three million children witness violence in their home each year.[2]

The age of most female sexual-assault victims is between twelve and eighteen years.[3]

The age of beginning female prostitutes is now between twelve and fourteen years.[4]

1. Moore, "Bump and Grind."
2. Clark, *Setting the Captives Free*, xiv–xix.
3. Marcus, "Confessions."
4. Ibid.

One underage boy or girl could provide one hundred thousand to two hundred thousand dollars per year for a pimp.[5]

There are between one hundred thousand and three hundred thousand underage prostitutes in the United States.[6]

My city (Portland, Oregon) had one of the highest underage prostitution rates in the United States.[7]

And I realized that these were statistics of only those who spoke out. I grieved because I knew that even though this happens under the sun, it happens in God's house as well.

Bogus, Bogus! Life can be bogus!
I saw a great evil under the sun . . .
A preacher spoke to his church and said that the women whose husbands were looking at other naked women in books and on the Internet, need to lose weight and become more attractive. That would make the men stop. I wondered why the men were not told to repent.

I heard that "boys will be boys," even when the saying applied to men rather than boys. I saw people sneer at feminists because they said that boys will be responsible and that men must hold them accountable. I wondered who actually empowered men.

Some men were worried more about their own sexual purity than about having compassion for all women.

Some women thought they had to be sexually appealing to men in order to feel good about themselves.

One in three men in my church fellowship admitted to having a sexual attraction to Internet pornography, and 70 percent of men aged eighteen to thirty-nine had looked at pornography once per month.

And I realized that people heard this and didn't speak up.

I grieved because the leaders in God's house didn't believe the statistics and said they weren't a problem.

Bogus, Bogus! Life can be bogus!
I saw a great evil under the sun . . .

5. Ibid.
6. Ibid.
7. Ibid.

A female political candidate cried in public, and her two male op-
ponents suggested that this was a sign of weakness, and that our country
needed a strong leader. I wondered if I could be an effective leader, because I have cried over some issues.

Women have given birth to children for thousands of years, but
men feel that endurance is a male quality.

Rape victims are retraumatized when people blame them for being
violated or don't believe that they have been assaulted.

Males perpetrate large amounts of violence against women, but we
call male violence a women's issue.

I realized that the majority of men are not violent toward women,
but we are silent. Yet women have always spoken out.

*And I grieved because it happened under the sun, in God's house, and
even though God has spoken, we do not.*

Bogus, Bogus! Life can be bogus!

Part 2

The Reality of Manhood

Coach

"Coach, who am I going to wrestle?"

"You don't want to know," I said.

"Yes I do. Where is he?"

"I'm not telling you. Don't worry about it," I said as I looked across the mat at the opposing wrestlers. They were sitting on the circle of the mat, straight, well disciplined, with probably not an ounce of body fat on any of them.

"C'mon, coach! Who is it? Tell me!"

"Look," I said sternly. "For the last time: it doesn't matter, and you don't want to know."

"I do! I do! Just tell me," he said.

"Okay," I sighed. "See the boy sitting over there third from the end?"

"Yeah," he said.

"That's him."

"Uhhhhh, I don't feel so good, coach."

"Well, Mike, you'll do fine. Just remember what I taught you, and be aggressive," I said as I smiled.

He lasted thirty seconds.

"Coach, why did you tell me who it was? Man, that psyched me out."

Knowledge is power—sometimes.

4

What Happened to Empathy and Compassion?

Empathy and Compassion: The Dynamic Duo

Empathy and Compassion in Human Development

In the previous chapter I mentioned that the missing links for the development of males from childhood to adulthood were empathy and compassion. Before we discuss this further, it is important to define both these terms.

Empathy is the ability to feel what another person feels. Usually one person shares with us feelings, emotions, and thoughts. Empathy causes us to feel what the other person feels. This is similar to sympathy, which is the ability to agree with what another person feels or to attempt to alleviate another person's suffering.[1] However, empathy is much stronger than sympathy, because it allows one to identify and connect emotionally with another person. When people share their stories with me that involve trauma, struggle, pain, fear, or suffering, empathy helps me to hurt for them, to emotionally connect with them, and to understand what they feel and are needing to share. Empathy is an act of becoming vulnerable with another person's humiliation and feeling

1. Thomas, *Moral Development Theory*, 157.

their pain. Empathy provides me with a logical and emotional reason not to victimize others.

Compassion, however, consists of the emotions one feels which allow them to have empathy. Usually when I hear the stories from people who suffer, I become affected (this is a type of trauma) and emotionally moved to hurt for another. Compassion is the emotion that causes me to feel and have empathy. Compassion and empathy both work together to help an individual feel another's pain and to act mercifully toward others.

Empathy is also thought to help individuals in their development of personal ethics. Martin Hoffman suggests that it is a central concern for the moral growth of humans.[2] Hoffman indicates that empathic arousal happens as a child develops compassion by maturing in five steps:

- I cry because I hear someone else crying.
- I cry because their crying reminds me of a bad moment in my life.
- I cry because I want to cry with them.
- We cry together as a way to communicate.
- I am able to put myself in their place and cry along with them.

For Hoffman empathy develops as the child matures and accepts the pain of others. However, the final two bullet points above are not automatic responses and require the individual to reflect on his or her experiences as they relate to the lives of others. In other words, adolescents or young adults develop empathy when they begin to think of others before themselves.

This is why empathy is an important moral virtue. Empathy helps the young boy continue to reciprocate in community and identify with those suffering in our society.

Empathy, Compassion, and Spiritual Development

The Gospel writers were very clear in expressing that Jesus was moved with compassion. Jesus lived in Palestine at a time when the Roman emperor, as a warrior, dominated the land with an iron fist. Roman emperors were typically not compassionate men. Tiberius was the ruler during the time of Jesus' ministry. He was a paranoid, perverted, and power-

2. Ibid, 155.

hungry ruler. However, the Gospel writers describe Jesus as an emperor, warrior, healer, and leader who was triggered by compassion. His motives for many of his miracles were compassion and mercy (Matt 15:32; Mark 1:41). In the Roman Empire the occasional practice of benevolence was expected, but the habitual practice of compassion, love, mercy, and forgiveness was not masculine behavior. The church believed that Jesus was the new man and the one who redefined masculinity in a culture of power. In a culture where violent men were heroes, Jesus became a hero without violence.

While some Christian men suggest to me that Jesus was a warrior before he was a nice guy, they forget that much of Jesus' ministry reflected his gentleness. He spent time with "nonmasculine" people such as eunuchs, women, children, sick and crippled people, and males who were common workers. In John's gospel Jesus is called a lamb (John 1:29), which was a sacrificed victim. In John's Revelation, Jesus is a slaughtered lamb/victim (Rev 4:6) who becomes the hero of the story. Even though Jesus was at times described as a warrior or victor in battle: these images did not mean to suggest he was violent. The king or warrior emphasis was as a contrast to the Roman warriors who conquered the world through a violent maintaining of peace (*Pax Romana*). Jesus, however, brought peace through patience, endurance, and love. Jesus the warrior was not violent, but compassionate and healing. However, he won greater victories than his Roman counterparts.

The life of Jesus was one that reflected compassion and empathy. The Apostle Paul emphasized the importance of these traits for the church in his letter to the Corinthian Christians. In 1 Corinthians 13 he wrote concerning the virtue love (*agape* in Greek). The church was struggling with immaturity, sexual abuses, prostitution, fighting, and arrogance (1 Corinthians 3–6). Since the majority of the people in the congregation would have been poor and from the lower classes, one can assume that wealthy members were causing the majority of the conflicts.[3] However, Paul wrote that they were immature and needed to grow (1 Cor 3:1–3). They were expected to be mature, but their fighting, arguing, and boasting (traits that were part of the "manly," political, and Roman culture) had stunted their growth. Paul wrote to these Christians that love or *agape* was mature, perfect, or complete:

3. For more on this interpretation of 1 Corinthians, along with other scholars' thoughts, see my book *The Better Way*.

> *Agape*/Love doesn't end. Prophecies will end, languages/tongues
> will cease, and knowledge will end. We have incomplete knowl-
> edge and prophecy, but when maturity comes, the incomplete
> will end. When I was a child, I spoke like a child, I thought like
> a child, I reasoned like a child. When I became a man, I gave up
> childish ways. (1 Cor 13:10)

The Greek word used in this text for "mature" is the word we typically translate "perfect" or "complete." Using this word to mean "maturity"
in 1 Corinthians 13, Paul challenged the church to grow up. When he was
a child he acted like a child. When he matured—became a man—he put
away childish things (13:11–12). For Paul, love/*agape* matures people and
helps them to grow to the "new human." In 1 Cor 13:4–8 Paul wrote that
love is patient; kind; does not envy others; is not rude, arrogant, easily
angered, or proud; does not rejoice in evil but in good; trusts; hopes; and
endures. These qualities made love desirable for the Corinthian church.
However, these were not traits of the violent warrior.

Any male in the Roman Empire would have suggested that Paul
was trying to create a church of sissies or at least a church that was countercultural. Yet Paul suggested that the key to normal spiritual maturity
lies in one's ability to practice love, patience, mercy, and other virtues.
In his letter to the Corinthians he modeled humility. Romans looked
down on those who worked with their hands. Paul described himself
and his team as common builders, farmers, slaves, and outcasts (1 Cor
3–4). He then told the church that he was their father (4:16) and would
rather discipline them with love and a gentle spirit than with abuse and
a stick (4:21).

Paul identified his ministry with humiliation, victimization, and
submission. When he wrote to the Christians in Thessalonica, he compared himself and his team to a nursemaid (1 Thess 2:6–12). For this
apostle, the strength of the Christian mission was its ability to identify
with the humiliated in society. The New Testament word we usually
translate "humble" also means "humiliated." Paul reminded the wealthy
Christians who met in Rome to associate with the humiliated or outcasts
in their church (Rom 12:16). This was an attitude or mindset: a willingness to become vulnerable.[4] This was also the reflection of a Messiah who
was victimized through the shame and humiliation of the crucifixion.

---

4. Clark, "Associating with the Humiliated," 62–64.

Empathy, Compassion, and Transformation

Christianity's power has always been displayed by its ability to liberate people from oppression and from being oppressors. Historically Christianity has focused on social justice, has identified with the marginalized, and has led the way in justice, healing, and freedom for many vulnerable people. Even though our history has been infected with the Crusades, ethnic cleansing, abuses, political control, and other sinful acts, the church worldwide has mainly focused on freeing the oppressed. In this ministry the church has identified with the mission of Jesus, who came to free the oppressed and seek and save those who were perishing (Luke 4:16–19; 19:11). In reaching the humiliated the church has identified with and helped them through compassion, empathy, mercy, and love.

It is this empathy and compassion that have empowered the church to love and accept all people. My family and I, our church, and many other people in Portland occasionally join Marshall and Leslie Snyder of Bridgetown Ministries in their Nightstrike ministry. Nightstrike began in 2002 with Marshall and Leslie's taking a pan of water under one of Portland's many bridges and washing the feet of those who were homeless. They would clean their feet, give them a new pair of socks and, in their words, "love the people of Portland." Over time people joined this weekly event to give haircuts, food, blankets, sleeping bags, clothing, prayers, and conversation to over two hundred people who come weekly to be loved by the many Portlanders who are there. What began with a vision and decision to love has grown into a ministry embraced by Portland's vulnerable people and political leaders, who appreciate what Nightstrike does for the community. When we come to serve, we hear people say, "This is what Christianity is all about." While our Christian history may sometimes suggest otherwise, our vision is to love and embrace people who need it most. In the words of Papa Roach, "The hardest ones to love are the ones who need it most."[5] Empathy and compassion are key components in the social, intellectual, and spiritual development of all people. These virtues also come forth in the ability of people to give back (reciprocate) to others.

5. Shaddix, "Carry Me."

Empathy, Compassion, and Entitlement

Pretty Fly for a White, Middle-Class Guy: White Male Privilege?

The four members of the Portland City Council were directly ahead of me. I was seated across from them with a small group assembled to discuss the Patriot Act and Portland's role in holding the authorities accountable. I was third in a group of four people who were to state our name, occupation, and opinion concerning this "Act." I do not agree that government has the right to torture, oppress, or create fear in the lives of people—even if they justify it by calling it "a weapon against terrorists." I was there because a wonderful friend, Dr. Herman Frankel, had persuaded me to reflect on the Patriot Act as a family man, a Christian, and a Christian leader in the community. I was disturbed over some of the language of this response to 9-11, and Herman's invitation forced me to apply Jesus' teachings to my local community.

It was a wonderful day. However, what I remember most was not the city council's response to our message. It was not the right I had as a citizen to address my local government. It was not the hard work that Herman did in preparing presentation booklets with our names and biographies and the necessary background information on the Patriot Act. These were wonderful. (Herman's booklet was very thorough.) But these acts did not stand out in my mind. What impressed me were the stories from community leaders who described their experiences of racism, persecution, and police brutality. I knew that Herman's roots as a Jewish man also reached back to years of injustice, oppression, and mistreatment.

The man on my left was African American. The man on my right was Asian American. The man on my left was a minister who talked about growing up with racism, experiencing prejudice, and suffering at the hands of people in power (corrupt people with corrupt power). I listened and remembered what it was like to live in the South and observe how cruel and insensitive some people could be. The man on my right talked about living in one of the prisoner camps where Japanese Americans had been held during World War II. He shared his family's suffering and struggle to overcome the stigma of living in one of these camps. Both of them not only knew the cruelty of prejudice, but they knew what happens when leadership does not rise above the sins of abuse, racism, arrogance, and oppression.

However, the man on my left and the man on my right appealed to the city council from their suffering, vulnerability, and oppression. All I could say was, "I oppose what is happening and I expect you all as my elected officials to also oppose this. As a minister I will be praying for you in this decision." That was it. No stories, no personal testimony, no experience.

- Just a white guy telling three females and an older man that they had better do what I elected them to do.
- Just a white preacher threatening them with the wrath of God.
- Just another person of privilege expecting justice because I can.
  - « It smacked of entitlement.
  - « It smacked of white privilege.
  - « It smacked of control rather than vulnerability.

I am white, middle class, educated, and male. I understand this. I have heard many leaders, including my dad, say, "The most disadvantaged person in our country is a white, middle-class male." I never believed it. Probably because I had an African American friend who was a deacon in our church tell me, "You won't know what it's like to be a big black man until you walk through a parking lot and hear the power locks click." That's when it began to register. Once at a father-daughter banquet that this friend of mine attended with his daughter, the main speaker painted his face black and sang a Louie Armstrong song. The guy was from the South, and this was post–Ted Danson/Whoopie Goldberg. I couldn't believe it. I hit the roof. I went to my friend and asked if this had happened.

He said, "I choose not to let it make me angry."

I chose to get angry. I preached about it in the sermon and shared that "We can't let this happen. This is the twenty-first century. We are supposed to be beyond this. Jesus' kingdom is supposed to have put this behind us." I thought that I was standing up for my friend but I didn't ask him if I should have done this. I did it because I felt I could.

Later I had a white elder tell me that I was overreacting. We had discussions concerning how African Americans are treated. He would say, "The most disadvantaged person in our country is a white, middle-class male." He really believed this. However, I learned some things about myself through that experience.

- I have never had trouble getting a job because of the color of my skin or my gender.
- I have never been mistreated because I am a man or white.
- I have never been disadvantaged because I'm a white male.
- I have rarely been denied credit.
- I have never had someone follow me and watch how I behave around children, in a store, or in a bank.
- I don't want to be like that elder.
- Because my friend chose not to let it make him angry, and I chose to get angry, he is a better man than I.
- I never did ask my friend what we should do. I assumed I had to stand up for him because he is black and I am white.

I demand because I have rights. I expect because people accommodate me. I have entitlement because as a white male I have been taught that a strong work ethic produces success. I don't know what it is like to be vulnerable because I represent the class of the oppressor. I am the author of control, and by expecting success I can trample others. It's hard being a white, middle-class male. When you are the author of oppression, you have to work to stay on top. However, when you come face-to-face with who you are, you realize that it is lonely at the top. It is scary at the top, and you feel guilty for why you are there. You have to find a way to kill your empathy and compassion on the way to the top, and in order to stay there.

I met Herman a few weeks before our city meeting. He had met with me in my office and shared with me his perception that the most commonly occurring major traumatic event in the lives of American children was parental divorce. He had been told about our abuse-prevention trainings and wanted to attend, but he wanted to share his insights on divorce and its effects on children. I felt that as a pediatrician and consultant to the National Institutes of Health, he would be open to our discussions concerning the effects of abuse on the family.

When Herman left, he said, "You have now shown me that divorce is not the most common major traumatic event for a child—domestic violence and witnessing domestic violence are even commoner and even more traumatic."

There it was. I had taught Herman the truth. He now knew. The least I could do was to go participate in his presentation to the city council.

I thought because I am a Christian leader, I was to grace the chambers with my presence, utter words of encouragement, and warn the politicians of the wrath of God. That's not what happened.

I met people who were oppressed. I met people who rose above discrimination. I met people who knew persecution. I met people who had persevered in a world that tried to keep them down. They lived in the real world, a world I was told had dealt with its injustice. They, unlike me, had lived their lives being penalized because of who they were, and what they looked like.

However, I didn't feel ashamed. I felt empowered. No one scolded me for being white. No one snarled at me for being male. No one persecuted me for being Christian. They thanked me for coming. Some said, "We need more people like you to join in this cause."

Then I realized, sitting by the man on my left and the man on my right, that my role as a white, middle-class male is to fight for the rights of the oppressed. It is to empower them to be strong. It is to hear their cries against injustice and to respond with them (not for them). It is to take the privilege I have been given and choose to empower rather than oppress. It is to be among the vulnerable of our population and rise with them. It is also to choose to not be an oppressor.

It's funny. Herman taught me more than I ever taught him.

Empathy, Compassion, and Pornography: Male Privilege?

Pornography is one of the fastest-growing and highest-grossing industries in the world. With the explosion of the World Wide Web, the industry has multiplied at an even faster rate than before the rise of the Internet. The proliferation of child pornography has also grown now that pedophiles can distribute, view, and produce this evil in the privacy of their own homes. Pornography is not illegal. Most pornography can be viewed in public libraries and in other places children visit. Young people have access to pornography simply by clicking a Web site and viewing free photos. All one needs to do is to open a new e-mail account, and the offers come to you.

When I was a kid, we lived near a university. At the end of the semester, we could spend time "dumpster diving" and find plenty of discarded pornographic magazines. We had to hide them from our parents but found it worth the work. Today, there are few barriers preventing young men from viewing naked females and males for free.

Many men whom I counsel individually or in marital or premarital counseling have a serious problem with pornography. They have smashed and thrown away computers or given them to friends because they recognize that they have a problem. Some purchase Internet blockers to prevent looking at these sites. Some ministries provide Web site blocks and accountability for those men and women visiting porn sites. We understand that it can become an addiction. We understand that Jesus calls it adultery (Matt 5:28). We know that it destroys marriages, families, dating relationships, and those who view it. We also know that more and more females are viewing pornography and becoming addicted as well.

However, opinions differ concerning pornography and males. In 1996 I remember reading an article in a magazine for retired people, in which a woman wrote that her husband viewed pornography and wondered if this was normal. The author of the article suggested it was healthy and normal for men to view this, even if they were married. Popular shows such as *King of Queens* and *According to Jim* suggest that the husband who views this is not affecting his relationship with his wife. I have heard presentations at abuse-prevention conferences suggesting that there is a difference between violent pornography and soft pornography. I have also noticed that there is a difference between how the secular community addresses pornography and how the faith-based community addresses pornography.

HOLY EYES

Faith-based communities, while doing powerful work to address pornography, seem to focus more on the personal struggle, purity, and self-control when resisting porn. While this is important and very effective, it seems to place the emphasis on the man resisting sin. Pornography then becomes an inner struggle and personal battle that one fights. Some suggest that the problem lies in a broken relationship with God, which must be healed and addressed in order for the man to feel whole. *He focuses on himself* in order to stop his addiction. Some suggest that the problem lies in a fear of women. The man must overcome his fear of intimacy, usually addressed by God, in order to heal. Again, *he focuses on himself.* Others suggest that the man seeks love and affection in fantasy and the world of pornographic images and false reality. He must live in the real world and develop relationships with others. This begins by accepting who he is. Again, *he focuses on himself.*

While I acknowledge that these have been effective methods of helping many Christian men, and other men, address their sexual addictions, I find that these methods are different from how the secular community responds. The secular community believes that the root issue in pornography, like many other issues affecting women, is the oppression of women. Pornography, sexual abuse, prostitution, intimate-partner violence, stripping, sex trafficking, and pedophilia all have this in common. They are industries that perpetuate the belief that females are here to please males. They also perpetuate the myth that males are brute beasts, by-products, and addicts of the sex-and-violence cocktail. I agree that this should be our method of addressing pornography with males.

First, the above-listed oppression issues are *controlled by males*. Males are the producers and males overwhelmingly are the consumers. In all of these sins, males oppress other human beings. While there are female perpetrators the larger percentage of oppressors are males. The pimps are males, the johns are males, the pornography producers are males, the consumers are males, the traffickers are males, and the pedophiles are males. The victims are women, children, and other males. Women and children are coerced, forced, or manipulated into doing what men want for the benefit of those men. One reason men struggle with pornography is that other males tell them that they want to see naked and vulnerable women. Another reason is that other males devalue these women and children and believe that they exist to please them. The women in these industries communicate what they are told men want to hear from them so that the men can receive gratification and pleasure. However, men have to choose to cleave to these industries.

Second, while these industries are real, they *produce a world of illusion*. The women are enhanced in the ways they look and act to satisfy the men. The women are expected to live in a world where men are afterthoughts, animals, and byproducts. There are no intimate, loving, and caring relationships in these industries. Even worse, the consumers provide no healthy type of intimacy for the victims. The men are consumers who take, and invest nothing into this relationship. The consumer is used by the producer, pimp, and slave trader as long as he has money. The women, who appear healthy, happy, and excited, are abused, manipulated, and hollow on the inside. The movie *Pretty Woman* was a myth. Most prostitutes do not come and go as they please. They are kidnapped or sold by other men. They are raped, tortured, and brainwashed by their pimp. They are transported to other cities, counties, or countries. They work ten to twelve hours a day, every day, and are given little food. They are taught to serve without question and live in fear of their lives. If they try to escape, they are brutally beaten, tortured, or murdered in order to serve as an example for others. If they survive the beating, they are sent back to work and isolated by the pimp and his other workers. They are discarded and left to wander our city as walking trauma survivors. In addition to all this, they are blamed for this prostitution by society. We assume that women choose to sell themselves for sex. Even worse, we glorify the pimp in our music, in our Halloween costumes, and by expressions such as "Pimp My Ride." Industries oppressive to women maintain a world of illusion where the consumer believes that his product actually cares about him, and that male and female coexist in harmony, honor, and respect.

Third, these sins of oppression that these industries perpetuate *destroy who we are as people in the image of God.* The consumer treats women as objects. His struggle is not a personal battle—it is a community one. He loves himself so much that he hurts another person, who is also made in the image of God. He continues to disrespect women and this is why he asks his wife to wear a wig, to dress in a shameful manner, to watch porn with him, or to mix pain with pleasure sexually. This is why he disrespects other women. This is why he likes to focus on himself. This is why he doesn't form healthy relationships with women. They are here to serve him. Pornography and the sex industry have taught him that he, like the ancient animal Enkidu, needs a good screwing to be a man. Who better than a woman to bare her breasts and spread her legs? However, this is not reality.

The solution is empathy and compassion. The struggle to resist pornography, stripping, sex trafficking, and other crimes can be strengthened if we teach men empathy and compassion. When we learn that prostitutes are slaves and oppressed people, we have to ask, "How can we take advantage of someone who is forced into this lifestyle?" My friend Zak, who is our recovery minister at Agape, is in the United States Navy. He has shared with me that when he and his fellow seamen went to port, men were taught to practice safe sex, knowing that there would be plenty of prostitutes in the city. As he became aware of human trafficking, he wondered if the sailors knew that they were further enslaving women—especially if they were there to fight for the country's freedom.

Empathy and compassion:

- cause me to fight to stop prostitution by blaming the pimps, not the prostitutes
- cause me to stop the johns who are consumers and to stop using the word *pimp* when discussing anything besides prostitution
- cause me to avoid porn, because it further enslaves women and oppresses them
- cause me to call pedophiles, abusers, rapists, and sex-industry consumers to repentance, to accept them, and to hold them accountable for their sins
- cause me to work to see women as partners in the kingdom, worthy of honor and respect
- cause me to emphasize healthy relationships with other humans, which encourage human beings to be the best they can be
- cause me to listen to the voice of women, children, and vulnerable males.

When Empathy, Compassion, and Reality Collide

When we allow only women, rather than men and women, to cultivate empathy and compassion, we should not be surprised that churches are filled with females. When we believe that a boy must reject the feminine in order to become a man, then we should not be surprised that so many churches and youth groups claim to lose boys when they are in their teens. When we believe that true manhood rejects the feminine, then we should not be surprised that many men do not attend churches. When we believe that compassionate women have an effect on the men they love, then we shouldn't be surprised when the men who love them make the decision to become part of the Christian movement. When we expect children to develop empathy and compassion, we should not be surprised that many churches have great children's ministries.

I read and hear often that men are the hardest to reach in Christian ministry. It's odd that most churches are led by men. If the church is at fault for not reaching men because it is too feminine, then it makes little sense why so many men send their children, especially boys, to church without them. I have been in ministry over twenty-five years and worked to bring children to church on busses, in vans, or by carpooling with other people. The men who stay home usually sleep in late (by themselves), watch a football game (by themselves), go fishing (by themselves), or work in their shop (by themselves). Why? They don't want to spend time with their children, they don't like to be in groups, they fear intimacy, they are tired from a hard week of work, or they think that they need *their* time. However, they have little concern that their wives are either in church watching the children or at home taking care of their needs. They have little concern that their children need time with dad as well. They lack empathy and compassion for others. They need the church to teach them how important these ethical values are to their lives as well as their families well being.

Not all men do this. However, I believe that we are missing the mark when we try to suggest that men do not attend church because it pushes the feminine side of their lives too much. If they were seriously concerned, men would not send their sons to this type of group. I am suggesting that the reasons most males avoid church are that:

- Christianity involves submission, something with which men struggle.
- Spiritual maturity involves practicing relational qualities and giving to others.
- Churches talk about being peacemakers.
- Turning the other cheek (Matt 5:38–40) represents a *non*passive, third option in a conflict (to stand one's ground) whereas many men believe in only two options for handling conflict: to fight or to run away.
- The narrow way is the way of peace and nonviolence (Matt 7:13).
- Being in church means being asked to make a sacrifice for others, especially for my children and my spouse.
- Men may be convicted by something they hear and may need to make the painful choice to repent and heal.
- Men may be encouraged to address painful issues that they have buried, and may be asked to talk about them.
- Christianity requires commitment, something with which men are uncomfortable.
- Christianity offers a loving relationship with a father, something many men may not have experienced.

I understand that there may be other reasons men do not attend church. Some men are only doing what their father did on Sunday mornings. Some had a father who was hypocritical, was abusive, or used church to control them. In the past some men may have been molested by clergy, by a church leader, or by another man at church. Some feel church is irrelevant to the direction they are choosing with their lives. Some just don't buy into the religion thing. However, the response of the church should not be to change who we are to reach men. The response of the church should not be to accommodate men or a cultural view of masculinity. The response of the church should be to do what it was meant to do. The church needs to confront culture and provide a safe place for transformation. The church must redefine masculinity and call men to a life of discipleship.

Spiritual Mentoring

First, *the church must model healthy male relationships*. As mentioned earlier, the Apostle Paul challenged the Corinthian Christians by modeling spirituality for them. He called them to imitate him and also suggested that he was their role model (1 Cor 11:1). Paul, like many of the ancient philosophers, believed that his role was to model the way his followers were to walk and live. Paul encouraged Christians to model his way of life; he led by example and acted "like a father" (1 Cor 4:16; Phil 3:16–17; 1 Thess 2:8–10). Paul also called men to be countercultural in the church by providing sexually for their spouses (1 Cor 7:1–5); loving and being faithful to their wives (Eph 5:25–33; 1 Tim 3:3–4), something few Roman men actually did; and being compassionate toward other females (1 Tim 5:22).

Not only do young boys need strong role models, but men who are approaching middle age need sponsors and a safe place to talk. Midlife crisis is a period of a male's life when he becomes skeptical of his past teachings and former patterns of life. At this stage, he begins to listen to his inner voice and do what he, not his community, believes is right. He questions his "moral compass."

For some, this midlife crisis is a time to reject one's moral compass and to chase inner urges.[6] For others, it is a time to reevaluate their

---

6. Fehrenbach, *Soul and Self*, 3–4; Hands and Fehr, *Spiritual Wholeness for Clergy*, 15–18; Balswick et al., *The Reciprocating Self*, 168–74.

course in life and to find a new direction, career, or vision for their lives.[7] However, during this stage of life, a male must have a supportive and safe group where he can talk about his feelings. He also needs a sponsor or mentor who can help guide him in this process while helping him to keep priorities intact.

Unfortunately the rejection of the feminine many times creates a sense of loneliness and pain in the transition from childhood to adulthood. This loneliness will continue in a man's life until he is mentored by others. Mentors who cultivate relationships and compassion can become powerful allies in helping men stay focused through this midlife crisis.

Second, *the church must develop males who can confront the cultural issues of masculinity and manhood, oppression of women, racism, and male violence.* Whereas women have taken the lead in addressing these issues, and have done well, men must rise up, work side by side with females and at times must step forward to protect vulnerable others in our society. Typically the church has been retreating from culture and the environment. In order to reach men, the church must be missional rather than attractional. This means that men need to engage men and their communities. "Spiritual men" who live in the *Man Box* will disrespect women, act abusively, view pornography, and ignore the suffering of the oppressed. They will be ineffective not only at reaching other men but also at helping the church become a safe place for transformation.

> How can violent men, many of who are Christians, engage in violence against women and children and not seek help from pastors and caregivers? They can do it because the churches have not identified male violence as a pressing ethical and religious issue. Why do many churches refuse to see male violence as a major threat to the health of women, children, and family and instead call for a return to "family values" (the male dominated, heterosexual nuclear family) as a solution to society's ills? They do it because of the church's patriarchal theology, which gives priority to the rights of men over women and children.[8]

The *church must also provide a safe place for people to heal from abuse, oppression, and trauma.* Rather than developing a men's ministry that reflects the masculine values of our culture, we must develop men's ministries that help men practice the fruits of the Spirit, which include

7. Fehrenbach, *Soul and Self*, xii.
8. Poling, *Understanding Male Violence*, 8.

empathy and compassion. Instead of calling the church feminine for working toward social justice, for empowering women and children to be safe and respected, and for stressing family values for married couples and parents, we must embrace the fact that these were and are the ministries of Jesus' kingdom in a culture of violence, oppression, and injustice.

Getting It Right

Those who are promoting the return to macho masculinity in the church seem to have misrepresented the values of God's kingdom. I find that King David is the typical model used for manhood. I remember when Lori and I would teach the young boys in church, ages nine to fifteen, we would discuss the "cool" war stories. David was a favorite because he was a warrior, loved God, and killed a giant. The Bible says that he was "a man after God's heart" (2 Sam 7:15).

However,

- David was not the greatest king.
- David was not allowed to build God's temple, because he was a warrior, a man of blood.
- Solomon was a man of peace.
- Solomon built the temple.
- But Solomon became caught up in sex, multiple wives, and idolatry.
- Solomon was the wisest and wealthiest king in the land but was still not the greatest.
- Josiah was the greatest. The Bible says that "there was never a king before or after Josiah who turned to Yahweh as he did—with all his heart, soul, and strength" (2 Kgs 23:25). He was the greatest king. Unlike Solomon, he cleaned up the city, removed the idols, and called the people back to God. He did this when he was a young boy.
- Josiah died in his only battle because, unlike David, he was not a warrior.
- Josiah was not a warrior, but he was the greatest king.

Josiah is a reminder that God's people are not always the warriors, wealthy, wise, or sexually expressive; they are simply people (and sometimes young people) who are willing to give God all of their lives. Cultural males will always struggle against the kingdom of God, because it calls for submission, peace, faith, and faithfulness. God did not ask the kingdom to accommodate them but for them to enter the kingdom, as a child, to be born again of water and spirit (John 3:3–5). This is humiliating, but it is the door to the kingdom.

Not only should we seek healthy models of manhood, but we must also realize that women have many qualities that we need as men. Beginning in adolescence, many males are taught that women represent behaviors and qualities we are to avoid. As we mature, we must regain these feelings, emotions, and behaviors that our male culture took away from us. While other cultures may view the passage to manhood as a rejection of the feminine, God has actually called men to a different passage.

"For this reason a man will leave his father and mother and cleave to his wife and they will become one flesh" (Gen 1:24). While we tend to use this passage in wedding services, I find that it has a broader meaning and usefulness. The rite of passage to manhood is not away from the feminine but toward it. The Genesis text tells us that cleaving to a woman is the rite of passage for the man. This not only applies to marriages. It suggests that males and females can live in harmony as a community. In a world that believed that the rejection of the feminine was necessary for male maturity, the biblical text intervened in time and space to suggest that men should connect with females in order to mature.

Earlier in the Genesis story, God created the woman as a "helper suitable" for the lonely man (Gen 2:18). The Hebrew word for "suitable" means "opposite" or "complement." The woman was the man's partner, friend, and companion. She was taken from his side (2:22) rather than his foot or head. The two were expected to live together in harmony. Males and females were created, in God's image, to live together as a team, as companions, as complements.

The man left his parents, which was a sign of maturity and transition. However, cleaving to his wife not only represented marriage; it represented a sense of intimacy that males and females were to have in community. Men and women should not only live in community, but they should coexist peacefully and be willing to share each other's strengths. While many cultures suggest that males must cut off the feminine and cleave to cultural manhood, the biblical text tells us that males must cleave to females for wholeness. Through empathy and compassion, men can learn valuable lessons that will help them develop and grow as leaders in God's empire.

Empathy and compassion not only allow males to live in harmony with females; these virtues allow us to have intimacy, respect, and honor together as a community. They also allow men to be better men. We learn to be in harmony with one another. Empathy and compassion motivate us to oppose oppression, misogyny, racism, and any industry that treats humans as animals. Empathy and compassion motivate us to love unconditionally, as God does, and to become emotionally and spiritually mature.

Keep Your Head Up, Son

A wrestler lost a heartbreaker of a match in overtime. He placed fourth. Third place went to state; fourth place stayed home.

His coach was a very well-respected coach among the referees.

As the boy came off the mat, he was crying.

The coach stopped him, put his arms around him, and hugged him.

Then he got down in his face.

"Look at me, son," he said.

The boy looked up.

"You've got nothing to be ashamed of, son. I'm proud of you. I'm telling you, you've got nothing to be ashamed of. Now hold your head up. Shake it off."

The boy nodded his head.

The coach was visibly shaken.

I thought that was cool.

I thought it was cool that he hugged him.

I thought it was cool that he called him son.

I thought it was cool that he was upset too.

I know why we respect him as a coach.

However, what would have happened if the coach would have hugged him and cried as well?

Would that have been cool?

5

Hearing Wisdom's Voice: Touching Our Feminine Side

Empathy and Compassion Revisited

The Early Years

As the previous chapter emphasized, empathy and compassion are necessary for the development of all humans, especially males. The problem is that cultural males are taught to remove "the feminine" from their lives in becoming adults. In their transition from childhood to adulthood, males are encouraged to reject and resist the further development empathy and compassion in their lives.

Empathy and compassion need to be reinforced as boys transition to adulthood. Typically boys are taught these two virtues from females and, sometimes, from other males. However, women become the main providers of empathy, compassion, mercy, and other traits necessary in the healthy emotional and physical development of boys and girls. Since women are important in this development, it is no surprise that a boy's first teachers are females. Daycare, nursery, Sunday school classes, and grammar school are places where children are frequently taught by females.

Unfortunately, males have the same capacity to teach in these early classes as females but are not as numerous. Low salaries, cultural expectations, and fears concerning adult males' interactions with small children prevent many children from having positive male sponsors in this stage of their lives. This is important, because many males can teach boys and girls empathy and compassion at this level.

Sad, not Mad

When I returned from my first mission trip to Albania, I made a pact with God. On the flight home, I decided that I did not want to be one of those ministers who went overseas, shared his faith and taught the Bible with others, then returned to the United States and left the evangelism on the plane. I asked God to lead me to further this work. I had never really heard much about Albania before the trip. Other than an occasional episode of *King of Queens* or *The Simpsons* (where Homer thought Albanians were people who were all white with pink eyes), I knew very little of the people or the country. I fell in love with both while there for two weeks. I had no clue that I would ever meet Albanians in Portland.

After a month of being home, one of the kindergarten teachers at my son's school had shared with my wife that she had in her class a Kosovar boy who spoke Albanian and very little English. We began to take the teacher to the family's home, and set up parent-teacher discussions concerning the boy. I also volunteered to help him in her class. When I would come to class to read for the kids, all the boys would climb on me and fight to sit by me. It was pretty funny. When I came to the class, I would often talk to the boys about being good for their teacher, parents, and others at school. Once I read a story about a boy who was teased by his other classmates. We began to talk about feelings.

"Is there anything about this story that bothers you?" I asked the boys.

They began to talk about how the boy in the story must have felt. They kept mentioning that the boy was sad.

"*Sad*," I said. "I don't think he was sad, I'll bet he was mad. You all ever gotten mad?"

The boys shook their heads. A couple raised their hands.

"That's right," I said, "I bet he was mad. That would make me mad. Would it make you mad? You ever been so mad you wanted to punch someone in the face? Now, what happens when we get mad . . ."

"Ummmm, boys and girls," I heard Miss Michelle say in her high voice. "Remember, we don't get mad but are sad. Can we tell Mr. Clark about that?"

Rebuked by a kindergarten teacher! I didn't look over toward her, but I knew she was just trying to make sure the boys were manageable. I was a little embarrassed by what had happened but didn't take it personally.

I understood her point. Years later, after going through batterer-intervention training, I came to realize that *mad* is really not an emotion. Anger is one of many emotions, but we males tend to focus on anger, which is one approved emotion for males.

- Someone hit me in the face. I'm mad.
- Someone stepped on my toe. I'm mad.
- I lost my job. I'm mad.
- I'm hungry. I'm mad.
- My heart hurts. I'm mad.
- My girlfriend left me. I'm mad.
- I lost my parents in a car accident. I'm mad.

Boys need to learn very early on that they have the capacity for more than two or three emotions. Adults have the ability to help them stretch and accept that God has given humans a multitude of emotions, feelings, and forms of expression. While young boys learn much of this from females, we men, who have become stunted in our emotional development, also struggle to help boys stay in touch with their divine image (and the many emotions) given them by God.

My concern for children at this stage is that it becomes confusing when empathy and compassion are reinforced in their growth until the teenage years. At that time, boys are expected to reject this behavior while girls are encouraged to embrace these morals as a definition of who they are.

First, *boys learn subconsciously that empathy, compassion, and other emotions are undesirable.* Usually violence, anger, and fear become methods of crushing these qualities that had defined who they were. Yet the boys also associate females, who access these emotions, with being undesirable. While they become physically attracted to females, emotionally males distance themselves from those also in God's image. This contradiction in their cognition causes confusion about who they are and will be as men.

If some cultures "drive the feminine" out of the boy, an empty hole is left behind. Male culture attempts to fill this hole with anger, silence, violence, and other behaviors that create loneliness, fear, and insecurity. This is why adolescence is difficult for young boys. Freud discussed the Oedipus complex, in which the boy resents his father because he is in love with his mother. However, the tension is not only from jealousy of the father and love for the mother. Tension also surfaces because the boy begins to side with the father as he seeks protection and validation.[1] This painful tension between loving mother and siding with father occurs as empathy and compassion (God-like qualities) are taken from the male. The loss of these important moral virtues creates a longing in the boy, but the male culture creates resentment for having lost these qualities. The boy has the capacity to learn from both males and females, but he learns mostly from other males how he should treat females.

Dykstra, Cole, and Capps suggest that boys who have been labeled losers at this stage struggle especially with loneliness and shame.[2] If they have not upheld the values of the *Man/Boy Box*, they are tagged early on as losers. This can be damaging for these boys. They need supportive presence from other males as well.

Second, *boys learn that those who model empathy, compassion, and other virtues are to be oppressed.* Since we are taught to remove (suppress) these emotions, we in turn desire to suppress others who freely express them. Women, children, and other males who are free with their emotions present a threat to us. This seems to be a major reason why many males oppress women, neglect children, and fear or discriminate against gay men or those they consider gay (called *homophobia*). This also may explain why so many males are also slow to practice compassion or to participate in furthering social justice and charity—for instance by helping the homeless, the abused, or street children; or by opposing racism. The suppression of feelings is manifested in oppressing others.

Third, *many males have difficulty embracing true Christianity because it upholds a Savior who is known for humility, submission, and compassion.* The response of the church should not be to begin ministries that do not reflect the humility of Jesus, but should be to "engage" and

1. Balswick, et al., *The Reciprocating Self*, 81.
2. Dykstra, et al., *Losers, Loners, and Rebels*, 7–9.

"retrain" men to reflect the glory of their Creator. We must acknowledge that complete submission to Jesus will be difficult for many men, because they live in a culture that seeks to crush empathy, compassion, mercy, and justice. In the Gospel of Matthew, Joseph heard that Mary was pregnant. The story tells us that, "being a righteous man, [he] decided to divorce her (or break off the engagement) quietly, and not expose her to shame," (Matt 1:19). By a normal definition *of righteousness* Joseph was "law abiding" and should have divorced Mary publicly and have allowed the community to stone her. However, Matthew suggests that righteousness has a new meaning. For Matthew righteousness involves compassion for the weak and vulnerable.

- In the Sermon on the Mount the righteous are the merciful, pure in heart, peacemakers, and victims (Matt 5:3–10).

- God the Father is mature and loves unconditionally (5:43–48).

- Treating others with respect fulfills the law of God (7:12).

- For a rich ruler to be mature/complete, he needs to give to the poor (19:21).

- Loving God and neighbor fulfils the law of God (22:37–38).

- The religious rulers of the day neglect the important points of the law, which are justice, mercy, and faithfulness (23:24).

- The righteous who stand before the throne of God and enter into heaven are the ones who care for the poor and vulnerable (25:37–46).

The church has been called to redefine masculinity and in turn to call men to practice the emotions and virtues God gave them. This involves a new type of righteousness. This involves a "new, righteous man."

Finally, *females are taught that males are incapable of being compassionate, caring, and sensitive.* Some females become overfunctioners, who believe that males are inefficient and in need of a caretaker. I taught at a Christian college for many years. I watched highly gifted, spiritual, and mature females do well in my classes. However, many of them married males in the school who were poor students, spiritually immature, and unmotivated. Some of the guys were popular, but I saw that they were not good candidates as husbands. However, once married, many of the men were "suddenly transformed" into leaders who, as poor examples, emotionally drained their spouses. The women were strong, and raised not only their children but their husbands as well. However, the women lived in a culture that taught them that men needed them, and that they needed to be needed. Unfortunately it drained them both spiritually and emotionally. Even worse, many of these men went into ministry or became leaders in our churches.

One way to change this warped image of Christian manhood is to find a way to connect the chain linking boyhood and adulthood as boys transition into adulthood. In order to do this, we must believe that empathy and compassion are necessary links to the survival of men. We also must find a way to embrace what women, as partners in God's image, can do in our lives. This is happening in batterer-intervention programs across the United States. It is becoming a standard that the batterers' groups include both a male and a female facilitator at the same time. Working with a man as well as a woman allows the abusive men to learn from the women how their wives feel about their behaviors and their violence. This is a bold step, but one that recognizes that men need a feminine voice during their healing.

Listen to What the Woman Says

One of my favorite books of the Bible is Proverbs. This book is not a book that contains wisdom circulated among families and handed down from generation to generation. The book has strong similarities to other ancient Near Eastern Wisdom literature. Proverbs is the product of a culture that used wisdom literature to train young men for service in the government, court, or community.[3] The use of the terms *youth* and *apprentice* (instead of *child*), the presence of terms exclusive to the relationship between schoolteachers and students, the teacher's appeal that students "buy wisdom" (Prov 4:5), and the mention of students in the king's court (Prov 25:7) all suggest that sayings in the book of Proverbs were written to young men being trained as apprentices. This training was designed to prepare them for leadership.

Wisdom literature was extremely common in the ancient world. Many countries used this style of literature to train scribes to become more efficient. Canaanite, Sumerian, Babylonian, Greek, and Roman texts suggest that the scribal schools were very strict, expecting students

---

3 For more information on the interpretation of Proverbs from this background, see my article "Schools, Scholars, and Students," 161–63.

to sit still, write, memorize, and obey the teacher. Many of the teachers used corporal punishment for those who were disobedient (usually called fools). While many men today suggest that American schools are not designed for active boys, they are much better than the schools in the ancient world.

The book of Proverbs, however, is unique in that a major character, wisdom, is female. The school father constantly appealed to the student to listen to Lady Wisdom. She is a jewel, a teacher, and a lover. However, it is odd that in other ancient Near Eastern literature, females do not have any voice in the teaching of the students. Rarely do goddesses (let alone other females) even speak in the wisdom texts. Females were typically not present in the schools of the ancient world. Yet, in the Hebrew Proverbs, Lady Wisdom was a major character and taught the young men concerning sexual purity, gangs, social justice, and integrity. She provided the voice of reason and compassion for these apprentices. Even more, the "school father" encouraged the students to listen to her.

> Wisdom calls out from the streets, in the markets she hollers; at the head of the noisy streets she yells; at the entrance of the city gates she speaks: "How long, foolish people, will you love stupidity? How long will skeptics enjoy being skeptical and fools hate knowledge? If you repent when I criticize I will pour out my spirit on you; I will make my words known to you. But I have called and you refused to listen, I have stretched out my hand and no one paid attention, because you have rejected my advice and did not listen to my criticism, I will laugh at your problems; I will mock when you are scared to death, when your are frightened and your problems come back on you, when distress and anguish come upon you. Then they will call for me, but I will not answer; they will seek me but will not find me. They hated knowledge and did not choose the fear of the Yahweh, would not listen to my advice and ignored by criticism, therefore they shall eat the fruit of their way, and become full of their own mistakes. Stupid people are killed by their rejecting the truth, and the apathy of fools destroys them; but whoever listens to me will be safe and at peace, without fear of disaster." (Prov 1:20–33)

It seems odd that in a world where women (including goddesses) were not encouraged to teach young Jewish men, this nation allowed the feminine voice to take center stage. I would suggest that Proverbs provides us with insight into the spiritual and ethical development of young males.

First, Lady Wisdom seems to encourage the young males to practice social justice, integrity, sexual purity, and compassion. As the young man cleaves to a wife (Gen 2:24), so the young men in Proverbs are encouraged to cleave to Lady Wisdom. King Lemuel's mother said that she is the noble wife/woman (Proverbs 31). The feminine is not rejected in this educational system but embraced as an important part of male development.

Second, while it is true that modern schools may reinforce the *Man Box* with boys,[4] I have heard that schools feminize boys, because of the emphasis on handwriting, sitting, and the like. However, ancient schools emphasized these same skills such as handwriting, copying tablets, sitting still, and other school tasks. Boys have for centuries been taught to focus and sit still. We should not assume that boys are being feminized in schools. We, like the school father of Proverbs, should encourage them to do well in school, to listen to the feminine voice of their teachers, to study hard so that they might "serve before kings" (Prov 22:29). Boys who struggle with behavioral problems in schools usually do so because of dysfunctional family dynamics, not because of the "feminization of schools." These boys do not have fathers who encourage them to listen.

Finally, the feminine voice must be present in the development of males. We as men need females in our lives helping us to become better men. Females need us as well in order to become better women. We are all created in the image of God for community. As Gen 2:18–24 reminds us, males and females complement each other. We are a team. We help each other become better people. Therefore, women are not our enemies; they are our partners. Males should not reject the feminine but embrace that nature as part of who we are. Being in touch with our feminine side means that we reflect God—the one who created us. It means that we become who we were created to be. It is the part of our life we embrace as we transition to adulthood.

4. Dykstra, et al., *Losers, Loners, and Rebels*, 92.

Father and Son: An Odd Pair

I was boarding an airplane, headed for a conference. As I walked down the aisle I scanned the seats to see if someone would be in the seat next to me. The line stopped, as usual, and I lost count of the seats. My eyes caught a man and young teen sitting together.

They were looking straight ahead.

The boy had his earphones on and was moving his head up and down to some beat on his I-Pod.

The dad was just staring ahead.

The boy had on a Megadeath T-shirt.

"No way," I thought. "He wasn't even alive when they were cool."

The boy had a baseball cap backwards on his head, with hair to his shoulders. He was probably fifteen.

His dad was wearing a country-and-western-themed T-shirt, jeans, and cowboy boots.

They both stared ahead.

Quite an odd pair.

The dad elbowed the son while staring ahead.

The son elbowed back without looking at his dad.

The dad elbowed back harder while staring ahead.

The son elbowed harder while staring ahead.

Then slowly smiles came across their faces while staring ahead.

"That's cool," I thought.

I found my seat and sat down next to an older lady.

I stared ahead and smiled.

I thought about my boys.

Part 3

The Future of Manhood

Humility

Humility = being of humble mind. In the biblical texts, it suggests that one is humiliated, oppressed, or associated with other humiliated individuals.

Humiliation = taking your wife to a Bon Jovi concert. Is he really that good looking?

Humbleness = the feeling you have when she says, "Oh, don't worry. I love you just as much."

6

Engaging Youth

Taming the Beast

It was a hot summer day in Portland. The sun was shining and the temperature was near one hundred degrees Fahrenheit, an unusual temperature in the Pacific Northwest. I was physically exhausted from this ordeal but knew I had to find more energy to finish this task with this beast.

I had driven my heels into the hard ground, pushed with my legs, and clamped my arms together. The beast howled and pulled forward. My grasp began to loosen, creating a small gap between the body of the beast and my chest. I quickly pulled my arms toward me and pushed my body backward with my legs. My bare feet slid on the ground and burned from the friction of the dry grass, dirt, and skin.

"I shouldn't have taken my shoes off," I thought, but I decided to dig in and let time, endurance, and power overcome the beast.

The beast screamed and lunged away from me. Instead of loosening my grip my body was pulled into the beast. I quickly recovered, dug my heels into the hard ground and started walking backwards. My legs were burning from the adrenaline and lactic acid, which made them feel rubbery and tired. Step, step, slide, dig, lean back, drive, step, step, slide, dig, lean back, drive . . . I had developed a rhythm. I seemed to be moving backward and pulling the beast with me. I was tired and wearing down. Last year I had lifted weights through the summer and had the strength to do things like this. This year I had elected to take the summer off and concentrate on running and gaining endurance. At this point I was questioning that decision. However, I knew that I could dig in, wait, and wear down the beast.

The beast was strong today, stronger than normal. It may have seemed that way, or it may have been that I was another year older. Each year this became harder and harder. I found myself wondering if I had made the right decision today, but there was no turning back. Once I locked my hands together and started pulling, I had to finish. This was a true test of manhood. To defeat the beast is always a test of our manhood (or at least we think that it is). That's why we play these games: we know that victory is sweet (no matter how risky it is). It didn't matter. I had to keep driving. Step, step, slide, dig, lean back . . . was now a pattern of breathing. I had a rhythm until I snagged the beast on a post. Almost naturally it grabbed the obstacle and began to scream. My momentum had stopped, and my feet slid on the hard ground. I had to refocus, gain my composure, and not panic. My best friend came to help me. She grabbed on and tried to pull, but the momentum was going the other way. As the beast screamed again, I decided to pull one last time. My hands began to slip and I saw it coming. This year we lost. This year it got away. This year we were bested.

No, I decided. I lunged backward jerking with my hips. The beast's grip snapped off of the post and I knew I had surprised it. I still had a few tricks and energy left in this old body and began to drive backward. I had done it. I had broken the beast's spirit. It was all too easy now. I arched my back, drove my head into the ground and hit a solid bridge like I did in my wrestling days. As I elevated my hips and drove with my legs, the beast traveled over my chest and was thrown over the edge . . . of the wading pool. He hit the wall and went in the water with a loud splash. His screams were muffled by the water. The little boys began to cheer and say, "Daddy got Nathan wet . . ." I slowly stood on my feet gasping for air and forcing a smile. We cheered and laughed. We told him not to squirt us with the hose, but he thought he was being funny. We warned him, threatened him, and even gave him the option of for-giveness, but he wouldn't listen. Fortunately we had taken his cell phone out of his pocket, which made the struggle last even longer. Now the victory was won. The beast was defeated, my best friend and I had taught our son that we were still in power, and the little boys saw that daddy is still "de man!"

However, the beast suddenly rose out of the water. He was sixteen, wet, and ticked. I was smiling, but he wasn't. I knew my time had come.

Are They Really Beasts?

I remember a similar scene when I was his age. My dad had attacked my little brother. I know that my brother could be hardheaded. I know that he didn't listen. I know that he would work for me but not my dad. I know that he had his issues. But I also knew that my dad had told him he had hated him since he was a baby. I know that my dad, who treated me as "the golden child," was not fair in how he treated my brother. That's why when my dad hit my brother with a rake, something snapped in me. I don't remember what I said, but I do remember it was threatening. There we stood toe to toe. My legs were shaking, and I thought I was going to get pounded. I was taller, faster, and in shape but my dad was a Vietnam vet, and that always made me think he could kick my butt. Unfortunately that's not what happened. I don't remember much of what happened, but I do know that I walked around with an attitude for months. My dad and I didn't talk much after that. He left my mom and my brother alone when I was around.

I spent many years thinking that he should have knocked me to my knees. I always thought he could have done that, but he didn't. I felt that because he didn't put me in my place, I was cocky, arrogant, disrespectful, and later became irresponsible. I felt that he should have and could have taught me to be respectful to my father. I felt as if I deserved to be beaten in a fistfight with my father.

My brother and mom felt differently. For them, someone had stood up to the old man. Someone had said, "Enough." Someone had put him in his place. He never told my mom the true story, and when she found out, years later, she was glad it happened.

I spent many years of my life preparing for that confrontation with my boys. I have heard many stories of the son trying to overthrow the old man and of the ensuing battles that continue because of that challenge. Guys would often tell me, "Sometimes you gotta kick your son's butt to show him who's boss." I think that as fathers we believe that the day must come when the young buck takes on the chief, and that it must involve violence. I wonder if we as fathers expect it, long for it, or just fear it.

I was talking to Lori in the car one day about our oldest son. He was fourteen and had been challenging me. My typical way of dealing with it was to ask, "Are you ready to challenge me? Are you ready to deal with that?" This time he hesitated, which meant yes to me. I shared with Lori that I didn't look forward to the day when we would have what I thought all fathers and sons had: that confrontation. I began to mention my dad, our confrontation, and how I needed to be humbled. I knew I didn't want to be like my dad. I didn't want a fight. My dad was in the wrong, and my son was different from me. Yet I still believed that a confrontation was inevitable. I expected this to happen. Even worse, the solution was supposed to involve violence.

Lori, who had heard the story too many times, finally said, "Why does it have to happen? You're not like your dad, and your son doesn't have to confront his dad for being abusive."

There it was: simple, and easy to understand. I had stood up to an abuser when I was a kid. I was not in the wrong. I didn't need to be knocked down. I needed to be supported. My dad had been in the wrong in how he had treated his family, and that is why conflict happened. He was wrong for attacking my brother. He was wrong for lying to my mother. He was wrong for not having the courage to admit to me that he should not have treated my brother that way. Fathers and sons don't have to have knockdown, drag-out fights; that's not normal. Even more, I don't have to look for the day to prove I'm boss. I can treat my son with respect and let him honor me. Maybe that is the key: the sons challenge injustice, not their fathers.

The Monster of Injustice

Children spend the first few years of their lives respecting, imitating, and responding to the behavior of their parents, caregivers, and family. Children enter this world completely helpless and dependent upon the community to provide for their needs. Human babies are the most helpless of all the creatures on earth and cannot defend themselves. These babies need nurturing, support, and love from those in their community. However, as children mature they develop skills.

Young children need support from their parents, sponsors, and community. This unconditional support allows them to feel safe. When I have coached sports for my boys and for others, I notice that even at as young as five years old, children begin to be labeled. Some are labeled good athletes, while others are thought to be losers, rebels, loners, or failures. Dykstra, Cole, and Capps point out that rejection, labels, and loneliness become defining characteristics to the spiritual awareness of young boys at early ages.[1] Boys who are *neglected* can overcome these feelings of shame and guilt when mentored by an adult. However, boys who are *rejected* have a difficult time even with a sponsor.

Boys who feel lonely also carry a sense of rejection. For Dykstra, Cole, and Capps solitude is the ability to be alone with God and oneself, but loneliness involves shame, rejection, and fear.[2] Fathers, instead of calling boys to reject the feminine, must encourage boys (and girls) to feel accepted. To reject the feminine is to cut off the emotional support of mothers and to quench an important ethic from developing in their lives. Fathers and other males must not only encourage children to be comfortable with themselves, but they must display empathy for, compassion for, and acceptance of who the children are.

Father Wounds

Over the years as a minister working with men, and as a man who has identified and begun to work with abusive men, I have noticed that the term "father wound" has an interesting set of meanings to many people. While psychology was criticized for placing blame on parents for many psychological conditions of their children, the father-wound issue has become an important problem in our country.

Statistics have been consistent in showing that many problems in the United States stem from absent fathers. Fathers who are emotionally and physically absent from their children do tremendous damage to these young people—damage lasting into adulthood. Those men who have been physically abusive to their children damage them emotionally and physically. Statistically, females who have experienced abuse become passive and withdrawn while males who have undergone abuse imitate their father's (or another male individual's) violence and disrespect for

1. Dykstra, et al., *Losers, Loners, and Rebels*, 7–9.
2. Ibid., 14.

their mother and other females. Men who are emotionally damaging to their children increase the children's anxiety, and indirectly cause them to experience shame, fear, confusion, and difficulty distinguishing between healthy and destructive relationships. Children who grow up with men who are emotionally absent also struggle with guilt, shame, and depression, and may develop at-risk behaviors. Men who are physically absent from their children's lives contribute to the children's feelings of loneliness, fear of abandonment, and shame. Spiritually, children in these homes struggle with self-esteem and a relationship with God (the Father).

While this does not minimize the mother's role in the formation of the spiritual and emotional development of the child, it does suggest that a male's neglect toward children is more damaging that his actual absence in the child's life.[3] While some children may have two parents in the home, a single parent can provide adequate support and encouragement to children. Single mothers have many times been told that their children are at risk because there is no father figure in the home; however, father figures who practice dysfunctional, addictive, and destructive behavior can be a toxic presence to the family. These women should remove men from the home who physically, emotionally, and financially threaten them and their children. Men who are not capable of providing emotional support and safety to children present a destructive presence to the family. However, when a father is absent *and neglects* a child, the young person can develop a father wound.

Father wounds are common in our country. When children are neglected or abused by their fathers, and other males, they suffer emotional scars. While both males and females carry these scars, boys are especially vulnerable to this problem. Boys who are affected by father wounds tend to become overachievers, workaholics, and compulsive performers. Other boys become very passive, and underfunction. Some try to fill this void through performance, recognition, and success. However, they set goals that are unattainable, and rarely find fulfillment and happiness in what they do. Others become depressed and find various methods for self-destruction, such as self-injury, at-risk behavior, drugs and alcohol, or other forms of self-medication.

Shame and fear of rejection drive underfunctioning and overfunctioning behavior. What is worse is that many of the men who suffer from

3. Ibid.

father wounds do not break the cycle, and continue to wound their next generations. Many males find their identity in their jobs and struggle to balance family time and time given to their occupations. They neglect their children because they have learned to remove their identity from "womanly things" such as being with their children. Others underfunction as fathers and further neglect their children because of their own shame. The tragedy of this cycle is that the pain that drives these men is the very pain that they inflict on their children.

My father was severely abused as a child by his parents. His father was an alcoholic and left his family while my dad was a young boy. My dad went to work as a teenager, dropped out of school, finished his GED, and went into the Air Force at eighteen. He worked his way up to becoming a pilot and instructor during the Vietnam War. He was a high achiever who started at the bottom and worked his way into leadership positions. Yet he too neglected my brother and me emotionally. I understand that he did better than his parents had done for him. He came to a few of my games, and I remember that he tried to be there for us, although he was very neglectful of my younger brother. However, I became the overachiever, and my brother struggled for years with shame, guilt, and some destructive behaviors. Unfortunately, shame drove both of us. I found out later, in high school, that my father had been married before wedding my mother and had had three other children that he didn't see. While he sent child support in the mail, he never visited them and rarely wrote them. Even though our father did better than his parents, the cycle of neglect or abuse was never really broken.

At my father's funeral, his third wife proceeded to tell me what a wonderful man my father had been. His daughter from his first marriage was there, also struggling from a father wound, and had spent years wanting to connect with my dad. She seemed to be at peace with this, and was also concerned that I felt negatively about my dad. (She is a Christian and felt that forgiveness was what I needed to express for him.) My dad was an atheist and had rejected much of what I had done as a minister. I had worked with many men who had fathers like mine and had listened to their frustrations. I had also worked with older men who had neglected their families and had helped some repent and try to heal with their children. I understood that this was an issue of repentance and healing, not of forgiveness and enabling. After expressing my opinion of my dad, how I felt he had neglected all his other kids, and how he treated his first two wives, the climate seemed a little tense. A few weeks later, my dad's third wife wrote me a long letter explaining how moral my father had been, and how I would never live up to the character and work ethic he had displayed. She also mentioned that I was immature and disrespectful.

My dad was emotionally abusive to all his wives.

His third wife was a counselor for sexual offenders.

How odd!

I saw something reinforced in my life as a child of a parent.

A person's value is not validated by their family, it is validated by their co-workers and those who see them on the outside.

My dad chose to suffer from his father wound. He became an over-achiever and displayed a strong sense of morals, ethics, and hard work in his career. (He was a psychologist.) However, he did not display this same sense of morals, ethics, and hard work with his family. He created a father wound in his family and failed to break the cycle. I understand that he thought that his being there was better than what his father had done. But neglect is more damaging for children than absence.

As a father of three boys, I have worked hard to break the cycle. I, like many father-wound survivors, am a workaholic. Like many ministers, I bring this into my ministry, a place where overachievers dominate and define the profession. It has taken years of work to be more than a physical presence, but I have had a lot of help. I have a wonderful wife who supports me, and whom I listen to for advice and honest reflection. Fortunately she was not at my dad's funeral with me. After I had expressed my opinion, she would have shared how my dad mistreated her as well as me. (My dad was a misogynist.) She would have spoken her mind to my dad's former wife when she had criticized me for being a disrespectful son.

My dad's funeral was a turning point for me. As a minister, I have been involved in helping young men to grow and mature as leaders. I have also worked with older males who are leaders or are seeking to be leaders. Some were wonderful men, who have been a great encouragement to me. The minister who trained me for ministry always encouraged me, supported me, and provided a listening ear. He would throw me in over my head, let me struggle, and swim out to show me an easier way to do the job. However, he reminded me that I *was swimming* and only needed some pointers to do a little better job. I have fond memories of older men and of men close to my age who taught me to be a better husband, father, and Christian. I can think of the many batterer-intervention counselors and trainers who have taught me many things about being a better husband.

Unfortunately many of the male Christian leaders I have met and worked with provided terrible examples of faith, manhood, marital faithfulness, and fatherhood. At times they have disappointed me. At other times they have neglected me, a younger man seeking guidance. Even worse, some have undermined what I have tried to do to be a good husband and father. This neglect and type of abuse have reopened the father wound. I served for eight years as a preacher in a church that had two retired ministers as active members. I can honestly say that neither of them ever came to my office to ask me to go to coffee and listen to how things were going. I can say that many times I went to them to visit and listen, but the reverse was not true. I understand that maybe this was how they had been treated by others during their years of ministry. However, they did not break the cycle of neglect. I have met many young ministers who work with church elders, and who have expressed the same frustrations. They too have the father wound re-opened. They too feel alone. They too feel neglected.

For me, the solution is not complex. I found that I had two choices. First, I could continue to surround myself with wounded fathers who wouldn't break the cycle. I could accept that this was the norm and continue to try to please these men. I could accept that this was as good as it gets and understand that I was lucky to have any type of male in my life. I could figure that if I couldn't beat them, I might as well join them and continue the cycle of distance and neglect. Many men do this. Many men are told to do this. Many men join the crowd and accept the inevitable.

Creating distance from the source of the problem is a second option. I began meeting with a youth minister who asked me to mentor him concerning a few issues. One was his frustration with other church leaders. We both uncovered his father wound, and I shared with him that I experienced woundedness as well. As we talked and connected, it became clear that he was mentoring me. His final solution was to leave the church, go to graduate school and study this more, and then find a church with strong, healthy male leaders. It was not long after he left his church ministry that I left mine. He had helped me to see that a second option was to search for other men who have broken the cycle. I have done not only this, but I have made it a responsibility to spend time with the male and female ministers with whom I work. I hope to break the cycle in my own life by supporting and encouraging them.

Being the father of three boys has also been a challenge to me. I have had to miss important conferences in order to be home on their birthdays, but I enjoy being with them on those special days. I enjoy knowing their teachers, coaches (sometimes the coach was me), and friends as well. I enjoy taking them to coffee or to breakfast and talking with them. At best, I hope that they can be a little farther along in breaking the father-wound cycle than I am.

I have found that father wounds are not confined to males. Many females carry father wounds as well. Some respond by becoming overfunctioners. *Overfunctioner* is a term developed by Michael Kerr and Murray Bowan.[4] These marriage therapists suggest that people need to have healthy differentiation (the ability to be alone and to develop themselves) in order to have healthy relationships. Those who become enmeshed in a relationship with another lose their identity and tend to be overpowered. The one with power, because the person is controlling and abusive, becomes an underfunctioner and "sucks" the emotional energy out of the other person. The other person then has to work harder to maintain a stable self and becomes an overfunctioner. The older term for this was an *enabler*, but I would suggest that enablers adapt and overfunction.

We live in a society that teaches many females to become overfunctioners. I don't blame many of the women, because I know what our culture teaches. It is always the responsibility of the underfunctioner to step up, pull equal weight, and work with others to solve the problem. However, this is not always encouraged or practiced. While we must continue to provide energy and resources to empower women, we also need to empower men to be what they need to be. Men are relational creatures, capable of living in harmony with the opposite sex. Men have value and can contribute much to relationships with those of the opposite sex. However, it will not only take strong men who are full of empathy and compassion to empower men. It will take courageous men and women to challenge the cultural views of masculinity and manhood.

---

4. Kerr and Bowan, *Family Evaluation*.

Engaging Young Males and Females

Empowering Whom?

We love our boys, but Lori and I have often wondered what it would have been like to have a daughter. When I talk with other fathers about raising sons and daughters, we discuss differences, similarities, and sometimes the benefits of boys over girls. Having all boys, I know that we will never have discussions about their clothes' being too tight, small, or revealing. It was not in God's plan or in the genetics of our relationship to have girls, but I think that they would be similar to boys.

However, men who have daughters tell me a common concern that I have heard often: "With my son, I only had to worry about one penis. With my daughter I had to worry about all the other penises in the world."

I wondered what they were saying.

- Are they saying that their daughter is incapable of making choices?
- Are they saying that all males are rapists?
- Are they saying that their job is to be a protector and to have control over their kids?
- Are they teaching their daughters to make safe and healthy decisions about sex?
- Are they teaching their sons to make safe and healthy decisions about sex?
- Are they assuming that I am not teaching my boys to make safe and healthy decisions about sex?
- Are they saying that their daughter will not be able to defend herself?
- Are they assuming that all men want their daughter?
- What are these fathers going to do on her wedding night?

Maybe I'm reading too much into these fathers' statement. Maybe the statement is a reflection of a myth concerning sexual violence, abuse, and power.

What do you think? The future of male-female relationships will require courage and a willingness to go against the flow of culture. First, *men and women need a safe place to communicate, to learn from each other, and to explore working as a team to fulfill God's mission.* Men need a safe place to learn to communicate and to work against their cultural definitions of manhood as well.

Second, *men and women must respect each other.* Assuming that men are incapable of communication, relationships, compassion, and creative thinking is not a fair assessment of the diversity that exists among males. Assuming that women are weak and represent qualities that men are to suppress is also unfair and destructive to women. Men and women must see each other as allies in a culture that can destroy the harmony and unity needed in our communities.

Third, *men and women must be able to model healthy nonsexual relationships.* Many ministers have shared with me that they do not meet with women even in public. While I understand that there is wisdom in making sure that a male minister is not alone in a private setting with a female who is not his spouse, I do believe that many women carry father wounds. Many women need to have healthy relationships with males. In the work of Agape Church of Christ with the homeless, street kids, and now those leaving prostitution, I see that many of the females need caring, loving, and holy male relationships so that they can see that men are not by-products, beasts, sexual monsters, or afterthoughts. Men should be able to respect women enough to model a safe and healthy relationship.

Many male ministers share with me that their concern about developing relationships with some females in their congregations or communities is that one will develop into a sexual relationship. This is the problem. Many men see opposite-sex relationships as being only sexual. This view of opposite-sex relationships is disrespectful to females. Other males have indicated to me that they are concerned about potentially facing false allegations of extramarital involvement. While false allegations can be made, statistically most accusations are true: If men cross the line sexually with women, they are pursuing the woman or are violating the woman's boundaries, and typically it is the male who rapes the female. Men must learn to respect females, and this requires them to use compassion, empathy, and respect for those created in the image of God.

Fathers must be comfortable showing empathy and compassion to their daughters. While we must encourage, love, and support our boys, young girls also need this support from males as well. When girls begin to physically and sexually develop, many fathers feel uncomfortable hugging or showing affection to their daughters. However, this is an important stage in the young adolescent girl's personal and spiritual development. Withdrawing affection is neglect, and it can cause her to experience shame, low self-esteem, and feelings of abandonment. Even though dad is in the same location as before, the daughter learns that males are distant and do not show affection. She also learns that she must initiate affection in her relationships with males. In addition to this, she learns that God the Father is also distant. Many women have accepted a caretaking role in their emotional and spiritual relationships, because they have been taught that males are not going to encourage them. Many females have become slaves in religious institutions, not because the Bible taught them to do this, but because they have learned that anything male requires female submission and service.

Young girls need to feel loved during the awkward periods of physical, emotional, sexual, and spiritual development. They need to know what it means to be loved by a male in a healthy and holy way. When they leave home, and if they choose to enter relationships with other males, they should seek males who give them the attention, support, and love that they need in order to become strong women. If they choose to be baptized into Jesus, they should see him as a loving and attentive husband rather than as an underfunctioner. They should also see this model of loving husband and father as the norm, not the exception. This also helps them to seek relationships with males who respect their boundaries and treat them with honor, as Jesus does the church.

If we are going to empower the next generation of men and women to live in right relationships, then we must help them to see that males and female are both divinely created complements, made in the image of God. We must show them that as males we have the potential to treat others with respect and to build healthy relationships with females as partners and co-reflectors of the image and kingdom of God.

Actions Speak Louder Than Words

In my first few years of ministry I worked in Bonne Terre, a small town in southern Missouri. It was a very quaint little town, surrounded by other small towns and within a county of thirty thousand people. Bonne Terre is about forty minutes south of St. Louis: and a convenient place for people to raise their family and drive to a bigger city for work.

Every year the arts committee in Bonne Terre would hold a *chautauqua* during July. This is a Native American term meaning "conversation." Actors were solicited to come to this weeklong festival and portray American legends in both their costumes and performances onstage. Over the years, we learned about many historical characters. Each actor would perform each night during the week under a large tent. In addition, actors would circulate in the community to show us how their character might feel about modern technology and the world as it was.

One character I remember was Elizabeth Cady Stanton. Stanton was an early women's-rights activist, abolitionist, and social activist in the late 1800s. She not only fought for women's rights, but she became a representative for women and religion. Since one of the members of the arts committee was a minister for the United Church of Christ in our town, I was invited to a special session when Elizabeth Cady Stanton would talk with clergy concerning the modern church as compared to the church in her day.

I was the only male minister present.

They let me begin the questions.

I asked, "What would Elizabeth Cady Stanton think about Promise Keepers and its work with men in the church?"

I was not prepared for the response I received. These women expressed many criticisms of Promise Keepers, of its effect on women, and of its reinforcement of female oppression by males. Three female ministers, an actress, and I were there, and I had a stupid look on my face. It was a good discussion, and I spent time defending the work that Promise Keepers, a 1990s evangelical men's movement, was doing to promote healthy families and racial reconciliation. Nevertheless, the group was not as enthusiastic, and expressed skepticism for what Promise Keepers was doing.

I had spent many frustrating years trying to teach males to be good husbands, fathers, sons, and compassionate men. I was barely a father but had for years known that churches were not calling men to responsibility. Promise Keepers, I felt, was doing something that I believed needed to be done. Men were being called to connect with their wives, to be sexually pure, to be involved with their children (especially if the fathers had divorced), and to become caring leaders in their cities and churches. While some in the session saw Promise Keepers as reinforcing old stereotypes, I saw it as the beginning to an awakening among men. I couldn't understand why the women in this group felt so critical of what Promise Keepers was doing. The more we talked, the more I understood and, I also believe, the more the rest of the group understood my point of view. It was a good discussion, and I left feeling that we had all learned something.

The next night we had joined the crowd to listen to the night's performance. Lori wanted to hear the speaker, and I offered to take our son, who was one year old, to the field behind the audience to run and play. I could hear the performance in the field and could watch my son at the same time. After about twenty minutes of playing with my son, I looked up and saw Elizabeth Cady Stanton coming toward me in her full costume. All the actors were fully dressed for each night of the performance even though they might not have had speaking parts. As I saw Ms. Stanton coming toward me I thought, "Great. I guess yesterday afternoon was not enough. I wonder if she is going to tell me I raise my son the wrong way."

She smiled as she came to me and said, "Hello Ron. I see that you have decided to watch your son so that your wife can listen to the performance."

"Yes," I said. "I wasn't as interested in tonight's speaker, and she let me listen last night."

"Well," she said. "If that's what Promise Keepers teaches men to do, then I believe Elizabeth Cady Stanton would approve of that very much."

Sometimes it is what we do that reflects who we are, what we believe, and what we are going to become.

7

Engaging Women

In Harmony with Women

In the beginning power existed.

- Power created powers.
- Power was horded.
- Power was dispensed.
- Power was taken.
- Power was rarely shared.

In the midst of this power, women found a way to survive, thrive, and come alive. Since the beginning of time, women have given birth, endured, and brought joy to the lives of countless men. Women have faced hardships, persecution, suffering, discrimination, and oppression but have found ways to bring hope to the next generation.

Over the years I have listened to stories from women who have survived physical, emotional, and spiritual abuse at the hands of their husbands, partners, or fathers. Women who have been raped, beaten, humiliated, sexually violated, or publicly shamed have shared these stories as part of the process of healing. Many of these stories have affected my wife Lori and me. Over the years, we have heard horrible events recounted as these women share their stories with their ministers. In many cases the stories traumatize us because of the graphic details, and because of the realization that human beings—males especially—are capable of the most horrible acts of violence toward other people. We wonder how so many women can find a way to survive after these terrible crimes.

Yet what is most amazing is how women have survived after millennia of abuse, oppression, and rejection by those like them, created in the image of God. The patient endurance and strong will over these years have given women the hope to make a better world for themselves and the children of the future. A man once shared with me that he felt endurance was a male characteristic. I asked him what he thought would happen if he made that comment in a class full of women, especially to those who had just given birth. He smiled and said, "I see your point." Women have proven not only that they can endure, but that they will be around for many more years to come. Thank God.

"You know, Ron, this problem all started when we gave them the right to vote!"

In my early years of ministry an elder made this comment to me concerning women. He felt that women in the church needed to be kept in their place (the church kitchen). I can remember Lori's and my laughing this off and, like the rest of the small church, realizing that this was just an opinion of a silly old man. However, what this elder said was a common opinion of many men I met.

Women have had to fight for voting rights, equal pay, better working conditions, respect, health care, and the right to be treated with fairness and justice. What is more, they have fought for the rights of others, including people of color, vulnerable people, children, and other men. Women, like their ancient mothers from the foundation of time, have looked out not only for their safety but for the safety of the most vulnerable in our world. They have stood to end slavery, abuse, oppression, and discrimination. They have shown many of us men how to be compassionate and caring individuals, and have encouraged us to join in the fight.

"Boys will be boys" has been the cry of many men who turn their heads to injustice perpetrated by other males. This saying does not empower men but encourages us to continue to consider ourselves byproducts, afterthoughts, or beasts. Yet feminists have empowered us by refusing to accept that "boys will be boys," and reminding us that "men will be responsible."

God's Call to Men for Women

God, not feminists alone, has called men to be responsible as well. As a Christian, I believe that the incarnation of God in Jesus Christ gives people not only a way to God but also a model for God's image. Jesus reflected God's glory, not only by what he said, but in what he did. He illustrated to humans that God was relational, held children, appropriately touched women, associated with outcasts, and challenged the wealthy to care for the vulnerable in society. He redefined righteousness and masculinity. In the Roman world, where sons carried on the trades of their fathers, this son of a construction worker from Nazareth moved his family to Capernaum and hung out with fishermen. He confronted the cultural expectations of eldest sons by developing relationships with the lower classes, suggesting that commitment to God's vision was thicker than blood relationships.

> His mother and his brothers came, and while standing outside they sent for him. He was among a crowd which was sitting around him. The messengers said, "Your mother, sisters, and your brothers want you." He said, "Who are my mother and my brothers?" Looking around at those sitting around him, he said, "Here are my mother and my brothers! Whoever does the will of God, is my brother and sister and mother." (Mark 3:31–35)

Jesus was not afraid to resist the cultural norm for the ways God's people should behave. The Apostle Paul also suggests that Jesus calls men to be countercultural in their families in the ways they treat their wives and children.

As a minister, I am asked by batterer-intervention and abuse-prevention advocates to talk about biblical texts concerning marriage and submission. Ephesians 5 is one text that they often ask me to explain. First, Ephesians 5 teaches that *God is a God who maintains relationships.* I find that in domestic violence cases, the victim (usually the woman) is blamed for causing the marriage to fail. We in the general public generally attack the victim because we feel that the burden to keep her marriage together falls on her. This is a misunderstanding of covenant. The burden falls on the husband. One passage that illustrates this is Eph 5:21–33, which is built around this fundamental principle.

> Wives, submit to your husbands as to the Lord. For the husband is the head of the wife as Christ is the head of the church, which is

> his body, and of which he is the Savior. As the church submits to
> Christ, so wives should submit to their husbands in everything.
> (Eph 5:22–24)

For some men, this suggests that women are expected to submit to them unconditionally. In some cases abusive men have argued with me that expecting submission is their God-given right, and that their wives are to submit. However, the section begins with Eph 5:21: "Submit to one another out of fear/respect for Christ."

Christian marriage is shared power. Both partners respect and submit to each other because they have a deep love for each other. Paul wrote this verse before he gave instructions to wife and husband specifically. Before reading the rest of the passage, men must acknowledge that a marriage entails mutual submission, and that each person must work with the spouse for the health and development of their relationship and family.

Ephesians 5:22–24 was not written for husbands; therefore, it should not be quoted by husbands to their wives. The brevity of this section may attest that first-century women were probably already submitting to their husbands. However, in light of evidence concerning Roman women, the plea for submission only recommends that wives continue to respect their husbands.[1]

Just as wives are to submit to their husbands, so the Holy Spirit is submissive to the prophets of God (1 Cor 14:32). God's Spirit can be controlled and silenced by human beings. Does this indicate that the Spirit or God is weaker than human beings? Submission says nothing about status; it is only an act of giving, support, and encouragement. Women and men submit to each other (Eph 5:21) in the ways God has shown them through love, peace, compassion, and joy. Men not only model Jesus through submission; through submission they also resist the temptation to let their culture define either their relationships with their spouses or their roles in their families.

> Husbands, love your wives as Christ loved the church and gave
> himself up for her to make her holy: by cleansing her with the
> washing with water through the word, and to present her to him-
> self as a radiant church, without stain or wrinkle or any stain
> but holy and blameless. In this same way, husbands ought to love
> their wives as their own bodies. He who loves his wife loves him-
> self. No one ever hated his own body, but he feeds and cares for

1. Clark, *The Better Way*, 75; Clark, *Freeing the Oppressed*, 73–74.